MERCEDES-BENZ
W123 series

1976-1986

Brian Long

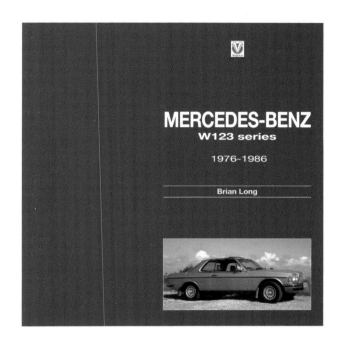

Essential Buyer's Guide Series
Alfa Romeo Giulia GT Coupé (Booker)
Alfa Romeo Giulia Spider (Booker)
Audi TT (Davies)
Austin Seven (Barker)
Big Healeys (Trummel)
BMW E21 3 Series (1975-1983) (Reverente)
BMW E30 3 Series 1981 to 1994 (Hosier)
BMW GS (Henshaw)
BMW X5 (Saunders)
BSA 350 & 500 Unit Construction Singles (Henshaw)
BSA 500 & 650 Twins (Henshaw)
BSA Bantam (Henshaw)
Citroën 2CV (Paxton)
Citroën ID & DS (Heilig)
Cobra Replicas (Ayre)
Corvette C2 Sting Ray 1963-1967 (Falconer)
Ducati Bevel Twins (Falloon)
Ducati Desmodue Twins (Falloon)
Ducati Desmoquattro Twins – 851, 888, 916, 996, 998, ST4 1988 to 2004 (Falloon)
Ducati Overhead Camshaft Singles, "The Book of the (Falloon)
Fiat 500 & 600 (Bobbitt)
Ford Capri (Paxton)
Ford Escort Mk1 & Mk2 (Williamson)
Ford Mustang – First Generation 1964 to 1973 (Cook)
Ford Mustang – Fifth generation/S197 (Cook)
Ford RS Cosworth Sierra & Escort (Williamson)
Harley-Davidson Big Twins (Henshaw)
Hinckley Triumph triples & fours 750, 900, 955, 1000, 1050, 1200 – 1991-2009 (Henshaw)
Honda CBR FireBlade (Henshaw)
Honda CBR600 Hurricane (Henshaw)
Honda SOHC Fours 1969-1984 (Henshaw)
Jaguar E-Type 3.8 & 4.2-litre (Crespin)
Jaguar E-type V12 5.3-litre (Crespin)
Jaguar Mark 1 & 2 (All models including Daimler 2.5-litre V8) 1955 to 1969 (Thorley)
Jaguar S-Type – 1999 to 2007 (Thorley)
Jaguar X-Type – 2001 to 2009 (Thorley)
Jaguar XJ-S (Crespin)
Jaguar XJ6, XJ8 & XJR (Thorley)
Jaguar XK 120, 140 & 150 (Thorley)
Jaguar XK8 & XKR (1996-2005) (Thorley)
Jaguar/Daimler XJ 1994-2003 (Crespin)
Jaguar/Daimler XJ40 (Crespin)
Jaguar/Daimler XJ6, XJ12 & Sovereign (Crespin)
Kawasaki Z1 & Z900 (Orritt)
Land Rover Series I, II & IIA (Thurman)
Land Rover Series III (Thurman)
Lotus Seven replicas & Caterham 7: 1973-2013 (Hawkins)
Mazda MX-5 Miata (Mk1 1989-97 & Mk2 98-2001) (Crook)
Mercedes Benz Pagoda 230SL, 250SL & 280SL roadsters & coupès (Bass)
Mercedes-Benz 280-560SL & SLC (Bass)
MG Midget & A-H Sprite (Horler)
MG TD, TF & TF1500 (Jones)
MGA 1955-1962 (Crosier)
MGB & MGB GT (Williams)
MGF & MG TF (Hawkins)
Mini (Paxton)
Morris Minor & 1000 (Newell)
Moto Guzzi 2-valve big twins (Falloon)
New Mini (Collins)
Norton Commando (Henshaw)
Peugeot 205 GTI (Blackburn)
Porsche 911 (964) (Streather)
Porsche 911 (993) (Streather)
Porsche 911 (996) (Streather)
Porsche 911 Carrera 3.2 (Streather)
Porsche 911SC (Streather)
Porsche 924 – All models 1976 to 1988 (Hodgkins)
Porsche 928 (Hemmings)
Porsche 930 Turbo & 911 (930) Turbo (Streather)
Porsche 944 (Higgins)
Porsche 986 Boxster (Streather)
Porsche 987 Boxster & Cayman (Streather)
Rolls-Royce Silver Shadow & Bentley T-Series (Bobbitt)
Subaru Impreza (Hobbs)
Triumph 350 & 500 Twins (Henshaw)
Triumph Bonneville (Henshaw)
Triumph Herald & Vitesse (Davies)
Triumph Spitfire & GT6 (Baugues)
Triumph Stag (Mort)
Triumph Thunderbird, Trophy & Tiger (Henshaw)
Triumph TR6 (Williams)
Triumph TR7 & TR8 (Williams)
Vespa Scooters – Classic 2-stroke models 1960-2008 (Paxton)
Volvo 700/900 Series (Beavis)
VW Beetle (Cservenka & Copping)
VW Bus (Cservenka & Copping)
VW Golf GTI (Cservenka & Copping)

Those Were The Days ... Series
Alpine Trials & Rallies 1910-1973 (Pfundner)
American 'Independent' Automakers – AMC to Willys 1945 to 1960 (Mort)
American Station Wagons – The Golden Era 1950-1975 (Mort)
American Trucks of the 1950s (Mort)
American Trucks of the 1960s (Mort)
American Woodies 1928-1953 (Mort)
Anglo-American Cars from the 1930s to the 1970s (Mort)
Austerity Motoring (Bobbitt)
Austins, The last real (Peck)
Brighton National Speed Trials (Gardiner)
British and European Trucks of the 1970s (Peck)
British Drag Racing – The early years (Pettitt)
British Lorries of the 1950s (Bobbitt)
British Lorries of the 1960s (Bobbitt)
British Touring Car Racing (Collins)
British Police Cars (Walker)
British Woodies (Peck)
Café Racer Phenomenon, The (Walker)
Don Hayter's MGB Story – The birth of the MGB in MG's Abingdon Design & Development Office (Hayter)
Drag Bike Racing in Britain – From the mid '60s to the mid '80s (Lee)
Dune Buggy Phenomenon, The (Hale)
Dune Buggy Phenomenon Volume 2, The (Hale)
Endurance Racing at Silverstone in the 1970s & 1980s (Parker)
Hot Rod & Stock Car Racing in Britain in the 1980s (Neil)
Last Real Austins 1946-1959, The (Peck)
Mercedes-Benz Trucks (Peck)
MG's Abingdon Factory (Moylan)
Motor Racing at Brands Hatch in the Seventies (Parker)
Motor Racing at Brands Hatch in the Eighties (Parker)
Motor Racing at Crystal Palace (Collins)
Motor Racing at Goodwood in the Sixties (Gardiner)
Motor Racing at Nassau in the 1950s & 1960s (O'Neil)
Motor Racing at Oulton Park in the 1960s (McFadyen)
Motor Racing at Oulton Park in the 1970s (McFadyen)
Motor Racing at Thruxton in the 1970s (Grant-Braham)
Motor Racing at Thruxton in the 1980s (Grant-Braham)
Superprix – The Story of Birmingham Motor Race (Page & Collins)
Three Wheelers (Bobbitt)

Rally Giants Series
Audi Quattro (Robson)
Austin Healey 100-6 & 3000 (Robson)
Fiat 131 Abarth (Robson)
Ford Escort MkI (Robson)
Ford Escort RS Cosworth & World Rally Car (Robson)
Ford Escort RS1800 (Robson)
Lancia Delta 4WD/Integrale (Robson)
Lancia Stratos (Robson)
Mini Cooper/Mini Cooper S (Robson)
Peugeot 205 T16 (Robson)
Saab 96 & V4 (Robson)
Subaru Impreza (Robson)
Toyota Celica GT4 (Robson)

WSC Giants
Audi R8 (Wagstaff)
Ferrari 312P & 312PB (Collins & McDonough)
Gulf-Mirage 1967 to 1982 (McDonough)
Matra Sports Cars – MS620, 630, 650, 660 & 670 – 1966 to 1974 (McDonough)

Biographies
A Chequered Life – Graham Warner and the Chequered Flag (Hesletine)
Amédée Gordini ... a true racing legend (Smith)
André Lefebvre, and the cars he created at Voisin and Citroën (Beck)
Chris Carter at Large – Stories from a lifetime in motorcycle racing (Carter & Skelton)
Cliff Allison, The Official Biography of – From the Fells to Ferrari (Gauld)
Edward Turner – The Man Behind the Motorcycles (Clew)
Driven by Desire – The Desiré Wilson Story
First Principles – The Official Biography of Keith Duckworth (Burr)
Inspired to Design – F1 cars, Indycars & racing tyres: the autobiography of Nigel Bennett (Bennett)
Jack Sears, The Official Biography of – Gentleman Jack (Gauld)
Jim Redman – 6 Times World Motorcycle Champion: The Autobiography (Redman)
John Chatham – 'Mr Big Healey' – The Official Biography (Burr)
The Lee Noble Story (Wilkins)
Mason's Motoring Mayhem – Tony Mason's hectic life in motorsport and television (Mason)
Raymond Mays' Magnificent Obsession (Apps)
Pat Moss Carlsson Story, The – Harnessing Horsepower (Turner)
Tony Robinson – The biography of a race mechanic (Wagstaff)
Virgil Exner – Visioneer: The Official Biography of Virgil M Exner Designer Extraordinaire (Grist)

General
11/2-litre GP Racing 1961-1965 (Whitelock)
AC Two-litre Saloons & Buckland Sportscars (Archibald)
Alfa Romeo 155/156/147 Competition Touring Cars (Collins)
Alfa Romeo Giulia Coupé GT & GTA (Tipler)
Alfa Romeo Montreal – The dream car that came true (Taylor)
Alfa Romeo Montreal – The Essential Companion (Classic Reprint of 500 copies) (Taylor)
Alfa Tipo 33 (McDonough & Collins)
Alpine & Renault – The Development of the Revolutionary Turbo F1 Car 1968 to 1979 (Smith)
Alpine & Renault – The Sports Prototypes 1963 to 1969 (Smith)
Alpine & Renault – The Sports Prototypes 1973 to 1978 (Smith)
Anatomy of the Works Minis (Moylan)
Armstrong-Siddeley (Smith)
Art Deco and British Car Design (Down)
Autodrome (Collins & Ireland)
Autodrome 2 (Collins & Ireland)
Automotive A-Z, Lane's Dictionary of Automotive Terms (Lane)
Automotive Mascots (Kay & Springate)
Bahamas Speed Weeks, The (O'Neil)
Bentley Continental, Corniche and Azure (Bennett)
Bentley MkVI, Rolls-Royce Silver Wraith, Dawn & Cloud/Bentley R & S-Series (Nutland)
Bluebird CN7 (Stevens)
BMC Competitions Department Secrets (Turner, Chambers & Browning)
BMW 5-Series (Cranswick)
BMW Z-Cars (Taylor)
BMW Boxer Twins 1970-1995 Bible, The (Falloon)
BMW Cafe Racers (Cloesen)
BMW Custom Motorcycles – Choppers, Cruisers, Bobbers, Trikes & Quads (Cloesen)
BMW – The Power of M (Vivian)
Bonjour – Is this Italy? (Turner)
British 250cc Racing Motorcycles (Pereira)
British at Indianapolis, The (Wagstaff)
British Cars, The Complete Catalogue of, 1895-1975 (Culshaw & Horrobin)
British Custom Motorcycles – The Brit Chop – choppers, cruisers, bobbers & trikes (Cloesen)
BRM – A Mechanic's Tale (Salmon)
BRM V16 (Ludvigsen)
BSA Bantam Bible, The (Henshaw)
BSA Motorcycles – the final evolution (Jones)
Bugatti Type 40 (Price)
Bugatti 46/50 Updated Edition (Price & Arbey)
Bugatti T44 & T49 (Price & Arbey)
Bugatti 57 2nd Edition (Price)
Bugatti Type 57 Grand Prix – A Celebration (Tomlinson)
Caravan, Improve & Modify Your (Porter)
Caravans, The Illustrated History 1919-1959 (Jenkinson)
Caravans, The Illustrated History From 1960 (Jenkinson)
Carrera Panamericana, La (Tipler)
Chrysler 300 – America's Most Powerful Car 2nd Edition (Ackerson)
Chrysler PT Cruiser (Ackerson)
Citroën DS (Bobbitt)
Classic British Car Electrical Systems (Astley)
Cobra – The Real Thing! (Legate)
Competition Car Aerodynamics 3rd Edition (McBeath)
Concept Cars, How to illustrate and design (Dewey)
Cortina – Ford's Bestseller (Robson)
Coventry Climax Racing Engines (Hammill)
Daily Mirror 1970 World Cup Rally 40, The (Robson)
Daimler SP250 New Edition (Long)
Datsun Fairlady Roadster to 280ZX – The Z-Car Story (Long)
Dino – The V6 Ferrari (Long)
Dodge Challenger & Plymouth Barracuda (Grist)
Dodge Charger – Enduring Thunder (Ackerson)
Dodge Dynamite! (Grist)
Dorset from the Sea – The Jurassic Coast from Lyme Regis to Old Harry Rocks photographed from its best viewpoint (Belasco)
Dorset from the Sea – The Jurassic Coast from Lyme Regis to Old Harry Rocks photographed from its best viewpoint (souvenir edition) (Belasco)
Draw & Paint Cars – How to (Gardiner)
Drive on the Wild Side, A – 20 Extreme Driving Adventures From Around the World (Weaver)
Ducati 750 Bible, The (Falloon)
Ducati 750 SS 'round-case' 1974, The Book of the (Falloon)
Ducati 860, 900 and Mille Bible, The (Falloon)
Ducati Monster Bible (New Updated & Revised Edition), The (Falloon)
Dune Buggy, Building A – The Essential Manual (Shakespeare)
Dune Buggy Files (Hale)
Dune Buggy Handbook (Hale)
East German Motor Vehicles in Pictures (Suhr/Weinreich)
Fast Ladies – Female Racing Drivers 1888 to 1970 (Bouzanquet)
Fate of the Sleeping Beauties, The (op de Weegh/Hottendorff/op de Weegh)
Ferrari 288 GTO, The Book of the (Sackey)
Ferrari 333 SP (O'Neil)
Fiat & Abarth 124 Spider & Coupé (Tipler)
Fiat & Abarth 500 & 600 – 2nd Edition (Bobbitt)
Fiats, Great Small (Ward)
Fine Art of the Motorcycle Engine, The (Peirce)
Ford Cleveland 335-Series V8 engine 1970 to 1982 – The Essential Source Book (Hammill)
Ford F100/F150 Pick-up 1948-1996 (Ackerson)
Ford F150 Pick-up 1997-2005 (Ackerson)
Ford GT – Then, and Now (Streather)
Ford GT40 (Legate)
Ford Model Y (Roberts)
Ford Small Block V8 Racing Engines 1962-1970 – The Essential Source Book (Hammill)
Ford Thunderbird From 1954, The Book of the (Long)
Formula 5000 Motor Racing, Back then ... and back now (Lawson)
Forza Minardi! (Vigar)
France: the essential guide for car enthusiasts – 200 things for the car enthusiast to see and do (Parish)
From Crystal Palace to Red Square – A Hapless Biker's Road to Russia (Turner)
Funky Mopeds (Skelton)
Grand Prix Ferrari – The Years of Enzo Ferrari's Power, 1948-1980 (Pritchard)
Grand Prix Ford – DFV-powered Formula 1 Cars (Pritchard)
GT – The World's Best GT Cars 1953-73 (Dawson)
Hillclimbing & Sprinting – The Essential Manual (Short & Wilkinson)
Honda NSX (Long)
Inside the Rolls-Royce & Bentley Styling Department – 1971 to 2001 (Hull)
Intermeccanica – The Story of the Prancing Bull (McCredie & Reisner)
Italian Cafe Racers (Cloesen)
Italian Custom Motorcycles (Cloesen)
Jaguar, The Rise of (Price)
Jaguar XJ 220 – The Inside Story (Moreton)
Jaguar XJ-S, The Book of the (Long)
Jeep CJ (Ackerson)
Jeep Wrangler (Ackerson)
Karmann-Ghia Coupé & Convertible (Bobbitt)
Kawasaki Triples Bible, The (Walker)
Kawasaki Z1 Story, The (Sheehan)
Kris Meeke – Intercontinental Rally Challenge Champion (McBride)
Lamborghini Miura Bible, The (Sackey)
Lamborghini Urraco, The Book of the (Landsem)
Lambretta Bible, The (Davies)
Lancia 037 (Collins)
Lancia Delta HF Integrale (Blaettel & Wagner)
Land Rover Series III Reborn (Porter)
Land Rover, The Half-ton Military (Cook)
Laverda Twins & Triples Bible 1968-1986 (Falloon)
Lea-Francis Story, The (Price)
Le Mans Panoramic (Ireland)
Lexus Story, The (Long)
Little book of microcars, the (Quellin)
Little book of smart, the – New Edition (Jackson)
Little book of trikes, the (Quellin)
Lola – The Illustrated History (1957-1977) (Starkey)
Lola – All the Sports Racing & Single-seater Racing Cars 1978-1997 (Starkey)
Lola T70 – The Racing History & Individual Chassis Record – 4th Edition (Starkey)
Lotus 49 (Oliver)
Marketingmobiles, The Wonderful Wacky World of (Hale)
Maserati 250F In Focus (Pritchard)
Mazda MX-5/Miata 1.6 Enthusiast's Workshop Manual (Grainger & Shoemark)
Mazda MX-5/Miata 1.8 Enthusiast's Workshop Manual (Grainger & Shoemark)
The book of the Mazda MX-5 Miata – The 'Mk1' NA-series 1988 to 1997 (Long)
Mazda MX-5 Miata Roadster (Long)
Maximum Mini (Booij)
Meet the English (Bowie)
Mercedes-Benz SL – R230 series 2001 to 2011 (Long)
Mercedes-Benz SL – W113-series 1963-1971 (Long)
Mercedes-Benz SL & SLC – 107-series 1971-1989 (Long)
Mercedes-Benz SLK – R170 series 1996-2004 (Long)
Mercedes-Benz SLK – R171 series 2004-2011 (Long)
Mercedes-Benz W123-series – All models 1976 to 1986 (Long)
MGA (Price Williams)
MGB & MGB GT– Expert Guide (Auto-doc Series) (Williams)
MGB Electrical Systems Updated & Revised Edition (Astley)
Micro Caravans (Jenkinson)
Micro Trucks (Mort)
Microcars at Large! (Quellin)
Mini Cooper – The Real Thing! (Tipler)
Mini Minor to Asia Minor (West)
Mitsubishi Lancer Evo, The Road Car & WRC Story (Long)
Montlhéry, The Story of the Paris Autodrome (Boddy)
Morgan Maverick (Lawrence)
Morgan 3 Wheeler – back to the future!, The (Dron)
Morris Minor, 60 Years on the Road (Newell)
Moto Guzzi Sport & Le Mans Bible, The (Falloon)
Motor Movies – The Posters! (Veysey)
Motor Racing – Reflections of a Lost Era (Carter)
Motor Racing – The Pursuit of Victory 1930-1962 (Carter)
Motor Racing – The Pursuit of Victory 1963-1972 (Wyatt/Sears)
Motor Racing Heroes – The Stories of 100 Greats (Newman)
Motorcycle Apprentice (Cakebread)
Motorcycle GP Racing in the 1960s (Pereira)
Motorcycle Road & Racing Chassis Designs (Noakes)
Motorhomes, The Illustrated History (Jenkinson)
Motorsport In colour, 1950s (Wainwright)
MV Agusta Fours, The book of the classic (Falloon)
N.A.R.T. – A concise history of the North American Racing Team 1957 to 1983 (O'Neil)
Nissan 300ZX & 350Z – The Z-Car Story (Long)
Nissan GT-R Supercar: Born to race (Gorodji)
Northeast American Sports Car Races 1950-1959 (O'Neil)
Nothing Runs – Misadventures in the Classic, Collectable & Exotic Car Biz (Slutsky)
Off-Road Giants! (Volume 1) – Heroes of 1960s Motorcycle Sport (Westlake)
Off-Road Giants! (Volume 2) – Heroes of 1960s Motorcycle Sport (Westlake)
Off-Road Giants! (volume 3) – Heroes of 1960s Motorcycle Sport (Westlake)
Pass the Theory and Practical Driving Tests (Gibson & Hoole)
Peking to Paris 2007 (Young)
Pontiac Firebird (Cranswick)
Porsche Boxster (Long)
Porsche 356 (2nd Edition) (Long)
Porsche 908 (Födisch, Neßhöver, Roßbach, Schwarz & Roßbach)
Porsche 911 Carrera – The Last of the Evolution (Corlett)
Porsche 911R, RS & RSR, 4th Edition (Starkey)
Porsche 911, The Book of the (Long)
Porsche 911SC 'Super Carrera' – The Essential Companion (Streather)
Porsche 914 & 914-6: The Definitive History of the Road & Competition Cars (Long)
Porsche 924 (Long)
The Porsche 924 Carreras – evolution to excellence (Smith)
Porsche 928 (Long)
Porsche 944 (Long)
Porsche 964, 993 & 996 Data Plate Code Breaker (Streather)
Porsche 993 'King Of Porsche' – The Essential Companion (Streather)
Porsche 996 'Supreme Porsche' • The Essential Companion (Streather)
Porsche Racing Cars – 1953 to 1975 (Long)
Porsche Racing Cars – 1976 to 2005 (Long)
Porsche – The Rally Story (Meredith)
Porsche: Three Generations of Genius (Meredith)
Preston Tucker & Others (Linde)
RAC Rally Action! (Gardiner)
RACING COLOURS – MOTOR RACING COMPOSITIONS 1908-2009 (Newman)
Racing Line – British motorcycle racing in the golden age of the big single (Guntrip)
Rallye Sport Fords: The Inside Story (Moreton)
Renewable Energy Home Handbook, The (Porter)
Roads with a View – England's greatest views and how to find them by road (Corfield)
Rolls-Royce Silver Shadow/Bentley T Series Corniche & Camargue – Revised & Enlarged Edition (Bobbitt)
Rolls-Royce Silver Spirit, Silver Spur & Bentley Mulsanne 2nd Edition (Bobbitt)
Runways & Racers (O'Neil)
Russian Motor Vehicles – Soviet Limousines 1930-2003 (Kelly)
Russian Motor Vehicles – The Czarist Period 1784 to 1917 (Kelly)
RX-7 – Mazda's Rotary Engine Sportscar (Updated & Revised New Edition) (Long)
Scooters & Microcars, The A-Z of Popular (Dan)
Scooter Lifestyle (Grainger)
SCOOTER MANIA! – Recollections of the Isle of Man International Scooter Rally (Jackson)
Singer Story: Cars, Commercial Vehicles, Bicycles & Motorcycle (Atkinson)
Sleeping Beauties USA – abandoned classic cars & trucks (Marek)
SM – Citroën's Maserati-engined Supercar (Long & Claverol)
Speedway – Auto racing's ghost tracks (Collins & Ireland)
Sprite Caravans, The Story of (Jenkinson)
Standard Motor Company, The Book of the
Subaru Impreza: The Road Car And WRC Story (Long)
Supercar, How to Build your own (Thompson)
Tales from the Toolbox (Oliver)
Tatra – The Legacy of Hans Ledwinka, Updated & Enlarged Collector's Edition of 1500 copies (Margolius & Henry)
Taxi! The Story of the 'London' Taxicab (Bobbitt)
Toleman Story, The (Hilton)
Toyota Celica & Supra, The Book of Toyota's Sports Coupés (Long)
Toyota MR2 Coupés & Spyders (Long)
Triumph Bonneville Bible (59-83) (Henshaw)
Triumph Bonneville!, Save the – The inside story of the Meriden Workers' Co-op (Rosamond)
Triumph Motorcycles & the Meriden Factory (Hancox)
Triumph Speed Twin & Thunderbird Bible (Woolridge)
Triumph Tiger Cub Bible (Estall)
Triumph Trophy Bible (Woolridge)
Triumph TR6 (Kimberley)
TT Talking – The TT's most exciting era – As seen by Manx Radio TT's lead commentator 2004-2012 (Lambert)
Two Summers – The Mercedes-Benz W196R Racing Car (Ackerson)
TWR Story, The – Group A (Hughes & Scott)
Unraced (Collins)
Velocette Motorcycles – MSS to Thruxton – New Third Edition (Burris)
Vespa – The Story of a Cult Classic in Pictures (Uhlig)
Volkswagen Bus Book, The (Bobbitt)
Volkswagen Bus or Van to Camper, How to Convert (Porter)
Volkswagens of the World (Glen)
VW Beetle Cabriolet – The full story of the convertible Beetle (Bobbitt)
VW Beetle – The Car of the 20th Century (Copping)
VW Bus – 40 Years of Splitties, Bays & Wedges (Copping)
VW Bus Book, The (Bobbitt)
VW Golf: Five Generations of Fun (Copping & Cservenka)
VW – The Air-cooled Era (Copping)
VW T5 Camper Conversion Manual (Porter)
VW Campers (Copping)
You & Your Jaguar XK8/XKR – Buying, Enjoying, Maintaining, Modifying – New Edition (Thorley)
Which Oil? – Choosing the right oils & greases for your antique, vintage, veteran, classic or collector car (Michell)
Works Minis, The Last (Purves & Brenchley)
Works Rally Mechanic (Moylan)

www.veloce.co.uk

First published in October 2015 by Veloce Publishing Limited, Veloce House, Parkway Farm Business Park, Middle Farm Way, Poundbury, Dorchester DT1 3AR, England. Fax 01305 268864 / e-mail info@veloce.co.uk / web www.veloce.co.uk or www.velocebooks.com. ISBN: 978-1-845847-92-0 UPC: 6-36847-04792-4 © 2015 Brian Long and Veloce Publishing. All rights reserved. With the exception of quoting brief passages for the purpose of review, no part of this publication may be recorded, reproduced or transmitted by any means, including photocopying, without the written permission of Veloce Publishing Ltd. Throughout this book logos, model names and designations, etc, have been used for the purposes of identification, illustration and decoration. Such names are the property of the trademark holder as this is not an official publication. Readers with ideas for automotive books, or books on other transport or related hobby subjects, are invited to write to the editorial director of Veloce Publishing at the above address. British Library Cataloguing in Publication Data – A catalogue record for this book is available from the British Library. Typesetting, design and page make-up all by Veloce Publishing Ltd on Apple Mac. Printed in India by Replika Press.

For post publication news, updates and amendments relating to this book please visit www.veloce.co.uk/books/V4792

MERCEDES-BENZ
W123 series

1976-1986

Brian Long

VELOCE PUBLISHING
THE PUBLISHER OF FINE AUTOMOTIVE BOOKS

Contents

Introduction and acknowledgements

The immensely-successful Mercedes-Benz W123 series – produced in saloon, coupé, estate, LWB and chassis-only form, with around 2,700,000 examples of the breed being sold between 1976 and 1986 – has a huge following today as a useable classic. Surprisingly, though, as yet very little has been written about the various models in English. This book aims to set that straight, covering the history of each and every variant from a worldwide sales perspective. Packed with contemporary colour photography thanks to the full co-operation of the factory in Stuttgart and the bringing together of various collections, the book will hopefully satisfy the needs of W123 enthusiasts looking for information, revive memories for owners past and present (the author included), and fill a gap on the library shelf for the many followers of Mercedes lore ...

Acknowledgements

As always, because of the use of contemporary photography as a matter of policy, these books cannot possibly be done without a great deal of help from the factory. As with the author's earlier SL and SLK books, I would particularly like to record my sincere appreciation for the services of Gerhard Heidbrink at Daimler AG in Stuttgart – a more helpful chap would be hard to find, and this book simply wouldn't have been possible without his unstinting co-operation and the kindness of those who work with him.

I should also like to thank Nils Beckmann and Joerg Rupp in Stuttgart for managing to drag me into the 21st century on the parts book front, Kenichi Kobayashi at Miki Press, the extensive research facilities at the Japan Motor Industry Federation (JMIF) in Tokyo, Rob Halloway at Mercedes-Benz UK, and Robert Moran and Christian Bokich of Mercedes-Benz USA. There have been many, many others, but to list them all would take another volume! But you guys know who you are, and my gratitude is for real.

As it happens, this title is helping to build up something of a Mercedes-Benz library at Veloce, as, thanks to our collaboration, we now have four SL volumes and two SLK sister books in print. There's another Benz one in the pipeline after this, and it's nice to see quite a few of them being translated into German.

The pages that follow also have a special significance for me, as an early left-hand drive W123 250 saloon gave me my first real experience of Mercedes ownership back when I was a boy, and maintaining it made me realize why the Stuttgart marque had gained its reputation for depth-of-engineering and solidity. Cars like the 450SE, 450SLC and an R107 300SL ended up in the garage because of this – it was a golden era for me, and always will be. All that remains to be said is that I hope that you will enjoy this book as much as I enjoyed putting it together.

Brian Long
Chiba City, Japan

1

The three-pointed star

The name of Mercedes-Benz, along with the three-pointed star trademark that goes with it, is recognized the world over as a symbol of prestige, exemplifying the highest levels of German engineering and quality. Before moving on to the book's main subject, it's worthwhile reflecting on the history of the brand, and what made it so renowned, to help put things into perspective ...

The Mercedes-Benz story begins with two pioneers of the motor industry – Gottlieb Daimler, and Carl Benz. Somewhat surprisingly, despite the fact that both were German-born, with both recognized as leading lights in the fledgling automotive trade, based less than 60 miles (100km) away from each other, they never actually met. Nonetheless, the coming together of the two companies they founded is what concerns us here, with the Daimler-Benz business using the Mercedes-Benz badge on the majority of its road vehicles from the late-1920s onwards.

Birth of the Daimler marque
Gottlieb Daimler was born in Schorndorf, a stone's throw to the east of Stuttgart, on 17 March 1834. Daimler didn't come from an engineering background (in fact, his father was a baker), but it was obvious from an early age that this was to be Daimler's destiny, for as well as learning Latin, he attended technical drawing school as a young boy.

Although he started his apprenticeship with a local gunsmith, as soon as his four years were up, he began studying engineering in greater depth, augmenting his academic work with practical experience gained in the field in France and Britain.

On settling back in Germany, Daimler moved around for a while, although his appointment as Technical Director of the Gasmotoren-Fabrik Deutz AG (founded by Nikolaus August Otto

The three-pointed star – one of the most famous trademarks on the planet...

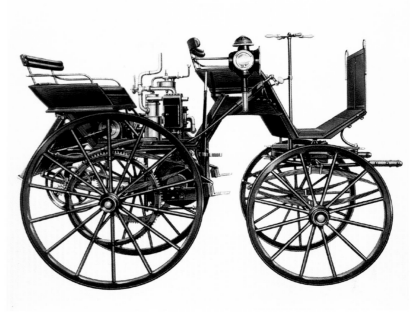

Gottlieb Daimler (left) pictured at the family villa in Cannstatt in 1885 with his wife Emma and two of his sons, Paul and Adolf.

Drawing of the 1886 Daimler Motor Carriage – the world's first four-wheeled motor vehicle.

– the father of the four-stroke, 'Otto-cycle' engine) in 1872 was an important step in his career, with Wilhelm Maybach (1846-1929), whom he'd first met as a colleague in 1864, already present as his right-hand man.

However, a rift between Daimler and the Cologne-based manufacturer grew in time, with Daimler and Maybach wanting to develop faster-running petrol engines that could release more power. Ultimately, in 1882, Gottlieb Daimler decided to go it alone and opened a small workshop at the back of his villa in Cannstatt, on the outskirts of Stuttgart, with Maybach working alongside to help nurture this new technology.

A number of single-cylinder, air-cooled petrol engines were duly designed and built, one being used to power the world's first motorcycle in 1885. There was also a four-wheeled horseless carriage, actually produced for Daimler's wife as a birthday present, which made its initial runs during the autumn of 1886. Within a short space of time, the engines were finding various applications on land, rails, water, and even in the air. After building a second car in 1889, this time powered by a water-cooled V-twin, it was obvious that Daimler and Maybach were

moving in the right direction, and investors soon started knocking on the door of the large new factory in Cannstatt.

The Daimler Motoren Gesellschaft (DMG) was registered on 28 November 1890, its purpose being to manufacture and market Daimler engines and related products. In addition, there was a great deal of licensing activity in this new and exciting field of engineering, with Panhard & Levassor of France being one of the first to sign up. There was also a company founded in America bearing Daimler's name (with William Steinway of Steinway piano fame behind it), and another in England thanks to the business dealings of Frederick Simms and Harry Lawson.

As so often happens once investors get involved, though, profits start to dominate decisions, and the desire to experiment usually has to be tempered with the sale of products to satisfy short-term requirements. Maybach was forced to leave the Cannstatt company due to a clash of policy, and Daimler's health was failing – a situation not helped by the internal conflict with members of the DMG Board. Perhaps not surprisingly, Daimler ultimately resigned from the company he'd founded in October 1894.

Carl Benz. Although for many years people believed he spelt his christian name 'Karl,' contemporary documents have proved that Carl is correct.

the Phönix, it was a landmark unit, and, following some political manoeuvring from Frederick Simms, the pair was asked to return to the Daimler Motoren Gesellschaft on new, more favourable terms.

Gottlieb Daimler died on 6 March 1900, although Wilhelm Maybach continued his work before becoming heavily involved with aero-engine production for the famous Zeppelin airship concern. After the Great War, Maybach marketed a short-lived series of luxury cars under his own name, with the brand being revived recently for a Mercedes-Benz flagship saloon.

Genesis of the Benz brand

Carl Benz was born in Mühlberg on 25 November 1844. The son of a train driver, after leaving school, he went to the Karlsruhe Polytechnic to study mechanical engineering. Following his graduation he moved around a number of firms, gaining practical experience in a wide range of fields, from building locomotives, to designing machinery and even iron bridges.

Joining forces with August Ritter, Benz established his own engineering shop in Mannheim, about 55 miles (90km) north of Stuttgart, in August 1871, but the partnership was short-lived, with Benz ultimately buying Ritter out. The small workshop was not a success, though, and Benz turned his attention to developing two-stroke engines (there were too many patents already registered against four-stroke powerplants) in the second half of 1877, with the first unit running successfully two years later.

By late-1882, the Benz engine had attracted investors, and Gasmotorenfabrik Mannheim was established, although Benz left the company within a few months of starting it, as the shareholders tried to influence things too much. For instance, Benz wanted to produce a motor vehicle, but a quick financial return on supplying engines was favoured by the majority of people. Having put up production facilities as his stake in the business, Carl Benz was left no option but to start again from scratch.

Luckily, on 1 October 1883, Max Rose and Friedrich Esslinger came to Benz's aid, helping to form a new company, Benz & Co Rheinische Gasmotorenfabrik, Mannheim. Not long after, many of the patents applying to the four-stroke engine were declared null and void, giving Benz the opportunity to start

Daimler and Maybach duly joined forces again (they'd remained close friends even after the latter left the DMG), this time bringing Daimler's son, Paul, into the fold, and between them they designed a 2.1-litre four-cylinder engine equipped with Maybach's innovative spray-nozzle carburettor. Known as

The Benz Patent Model 3, first seen in 1886, with Carl Benz seen driving, and Josef Brecht beside him – a close friend and business associate, who was later a director of the Benz & Cie concern. This vehicle, and the Daimler from the same year, provided the foundation stone for today's motor industry.

developing a new, fast-running powerplant based on the Otto-cycle. By 29 January 1886, a patent had been filed on the world's first, purpose-built vehicle to be powered by a petrol engine – the three-wheeled Benz Patent Motorwagon. Refinements were made, and the car was duly put into series production, the 'Model 3' version thereby providing the foundation stone for the automotive industry.

Ironically, in the spring of 1890, despite Benz & Co being Germany's second largest engine manufacturer, Carl Benz once again found himself alone in business. But new partners were promptly found, and Benz continued to innovate, with four-wheeled cars being produced, new steering systems designed, and the horizontally-opposed (boxer) engine being developed, amongst other things.

The four-wheeled Velo, introduced in April 1894, was a huge commercial success by the standards of the day (around 1200 were built), and a new company, Benz & Cie AG, was registered in May 1899. However, the people running the firm wanted to compete with a flood of cheaper machines built in France. Disillusioned, Benz resigned in January 1903.

A new century, a new age

Daimler and Benz were still rivals at the turn of the century, the companies bearing their names fighting in the showrooms graced by the rich and famous, and in the long-distance races and hillclimbs of Europe.

As it happens, the competition link provided the birth of the Mercedes brand. Shortly after Gottlieb Daimler passed away, Emil Jellinek (an Austrian businessman who, among other things, sold Daimlers to wealthy clients in the south of France) entered a couple of Daimlers in the Nice-La Turbie hillclimb using his pseudonym 'Mercédès' – the name of his daughter.

Following the fatal accident of one of the drivers, Jellinek proposed a number of changes that would not only improve safety, but also enhance the sporting nature of the vehicles to satisfy the needs of his customers. He requested a reduction in weight, a lower body, and a longer wheelbase in order to cope with the greater power outputs he outlined. Jellinek promised to purchase a large number of these vehicles in return for distribution rights in France, Belgium, the Austro-Hungarian Empire and America, but also requested that they carry the 'Mercédès' badge.

The four-cylinder Daimler Phoenix, in production from 1898 to 1902, but ably superceded by the more modern Mercédès line-up.

A 40hp Mercédès-Simplex that broke the record for the Nice-La Turbie hillclimb in April 1902. By this time, Daimler in Coventry, England, had long since found its own direction in terms of design and manufacturing, but William Steinway, of piano fame, would soon start building Mercédès cars under licence in the States.

A deal was struck on 2 April 1900, and Wilhelm Maybach set about designing the first Mercédès in conjunction with Paul Daimler without delay. By the end of the year, Jellinek had taken delivery of the first of the line – a racing car that ultimately provided the foundation stone for the modern automobile, with a low-slung, pressed steel chassis frame playing host to a 5.9-litre, 35hp engine cooled by a honeycomb radiator, and a gate for the gearchange.

The Mercédès was raced with a great deal of success, and many variations were produced for regular road use, from an 8/11hp version all the way up to a 9.2-litre 60hp model. The Mercédès (the name being registered as a trademark by the DMG in 1902), set the standard for the day in the high-class car market, and was built under licence by numerous manufacturers.

Luckily, the DMG Board had made preparations for expansion in advance of its commercial success, buying a large piece of land in Untertürkheim on the eastern edge of Stuttgart in August 1900. This would duly become the spiritual home of Mercedes-Benz, becoming operational at the end of 1903.

Six-cylinder engines followed in 1906, and there was a limited run of Knight sleeve-valve models just before the First World War. Meanwhile, the famous three-pointed star had been registered as a trademark, with approval eventually coming in February 1911. The three arms within the three-pointed star represent the land, sea and air, and indeed each has been conquered in the Stuttgart company's own inimitable way over the years; the outer ring was first added in 1921.

Shortly after the Great War, when the conflict had if nothing else allowed technology, metallurgy and production techniques to make great advances, the first supercharged Mercédès made its debut, and on 30 April 1923, Ferdinand Porsche was drafted in from Austro-Daimler to replace Paul Daimler as Chief Engineer, bringing overhead camshafts and front-wheel brakes to the marque in a series of exceptionally elegant supercharged models.

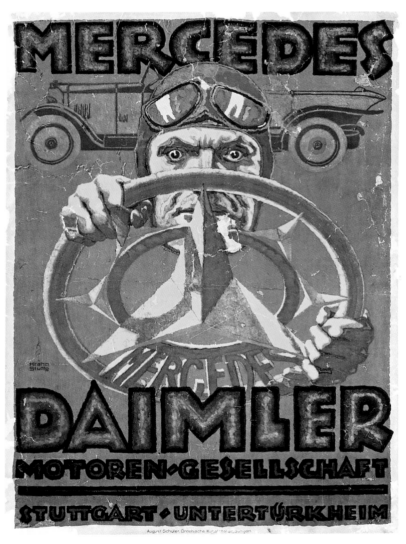

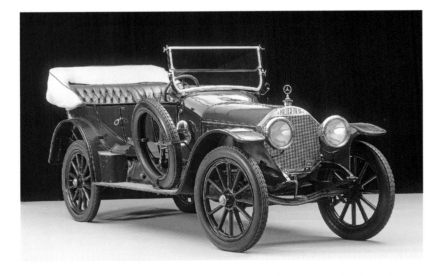

A chain-drive Mercédès 22/40hp model from 1910, built at the Daimler Motoren Gesellschaft (DMG) works at Untertürkheim.

A magnificent Mercédès poster issued to coincide with the 1921 Berlin Motor Show. The Mercédès marque was highly successful in top class competition at this time.

The rather conventional but nonetheless important Benz 10/12hp Parsifal making its international debut at the 1902 Paris Salon. With a propshaft delivering power from the front-mounted twin to the rear wheels, it moved the Benz brand into a new era.

In the meantime, Benz & Cie AG came to the fore, modernizing its range via conventional two- and four-cylinder cars designed by Marius Barbarou. The move towards reasonably-priced machines allowed the Benz business to clock up world-leading sales of around 600 units a year at the turn of the century, but the policy was out of step with that of Carl Benz himself. As mentioned earlier, he gave up his post as Chief Engineer, although he did remain on the Supervisory Board until his death on 4 April 1929.

While all this political manoeuvering was going on, Carl Benz had formed a new company with his son, Eugen, on 9 June 1906, called C Benz Söhne. By 1908, it had turned to car production after demand for the gas engines they were building fell off. This particular business, based in Ladenburg, to the east of Mannheim, was duly handed over to Eugen and his younger brother, Richard, in 1912. However, given the problems associated with the German economy following the First World War, the firm officially stopped building cars in 1923.

Benz & Cie AG continued down a safe path with its vehicle line-up; a racing programme, and diesel engine and aero-engine development going on in the background. The Benz badge gained its laurel wreath in the summer of 1909, and a take-over of Süddeutsche Automobilfabrik Gaggenau GmbH not long after provided Benz with a ready-made line of commercial vehicles.

Meanwhile, from 1910, Hans Nibel had been put in charge of car design. Interestingly, Nibel's own love of racing (he'd been involved with the machine that formed the basis for the 'Blitzen Benz' record breaker) spawned a number of competition cars, and the Benz marque duly found favour with a wealthy clientele. One of the most ardent supporters of the brand was Prince Henry of Prussia – the brother of Kaiser Wilhelm II.

Benz introduced its first six-cylinder powerplant in 1914. This was actually an aero-engine, but the company stuck almost exclusively to straight-sixes for its road cars following the First World War. During the war years, Benz had produced some

A six-cylinder 16/50hp Benz limousine from 1921. This car was actually given the Mercedes-Benz name after the merger, although it only continued in the revised line-up until 1927.

magnificent aero-engines, including four-valve per cylinder units and a V12 prototype. It also emerged from the conflict as a leading light in the field of diesel technology.

The merger of two great houses

Following the end of the First World War, Germany suffered greatly at the hands of hyperinflation. Such conditions are naturally far from ideal for manufacturers of expensive goods,

A Benz pictured in Johannesburg in 1910, when Prince Lowenstein-Wittgenstein was the South African importer. As well as having a strong following abroad, the Benz marque was – like its DMG rival – also very active in competition on both sides of the Atlantic.

and with Deutsche Bank holding a huge amount of shares in both the Daimler Motoren Gesellschaft and Benz & Cie. AG, it was decided that a syndicate be formed in order to save production costs. An agreement of mutual interest was duly signed on 1 May 1924, with a full merger and the birth of Daimler-Benz AG taking place on 28 June 1926.

Although the company was known as Daimler-Benz, the cars were marketed using the Mercedes-Benz name, with Mercedes officially losing the accents along the way. Only two Benz models made it into the Mercedes-Benz passenger car programme, and both were gone by 1927. A new badge, combining the Mercedes-Benz name, Benz laurels and the familiar three-pointed star had been registered soon after the merger.

There were straight-eights from October 1928, and following the departure of Ferdinand Porsche at the end of the year, Hans Nibel took over sole responsibility as the company's Chief Engineer; the pair had been sharing the post since the merger.

Despite the difficult financial climate left in the wake of the Wall Street Crash, the marque entered the mid-1930s with some magnificent creations, with the SS and SSK giving way to the 500K and 540K. By this time, the company was producing a range of vehicles that went from modest 1.3-litre saloons, with its NA four at the rear, all the way up to 7.7-litre supercharged eights with their glamorous coachbuilt bodies.

Meanwhile, 1934 had witnessed the debut of the first of the Silver Arrows – the ultra-modern W25 Grand Prix car. This was followed by a string of successful models that combined with the might of the Auto Union team to put Germany at the forefront of the motorsport scene until the outbreak of the Second World War. Record breakers were also built, based on the GP cars, and brought the new Autobahn network into use in a rather

A domestic advert proclaiming the merger of two of the greatest names in the German car industry, if not the world.

Racing hero Rudolf Caracciola pictured with his SSK at the 1930 Mille Miglia. Caracciola and his partner for the Italian classic, Christian Werner, duly went on to finish the race in sixth (first in Class).

A 500K Cabriolet C of 1934 vintage.

Although the Stuttgart maker was famous for its glamorous road cars and racing machinery during the late 1930s, most of the company's income came from bread-and-butter cars like this six-cylinder W153 230, built between 1938 and 1943. The similar-looking four-cylinder 170 series was revived when war ended to get the production lines rolling again after the conflict.

unexpected fashion – the straight, level roads being perfect for the challenge to find the fastest man on Earth.

Following Hans Nibel's death in 1934, Max Sailer took over as the head of design and R&D. Sailer had been associated with the Stuttgart marque for decades, most visibly as a racing driver of note in the vintage era. During Sailer's watch, products as diverse as the 540K, the 170V and 170H, and the 260D (the world's first diesel series-production passenger car) were released. The factory also built the first batch of VW30 test vehicles during the spring of 1937 – the ancestors of the Volkswagen Beetle.

Then, of course, 1939 brought with it conflict, first in Europe, and then on a global scale. Virtually all the historic Untertürkheim factory had been destroyed during successive Allied bombing runs in November 1943 and September 1944. Other plants were either destroyed or badly damaged, too, making it difficult for Daimler-Benz to bounce back once the hostilities came to an end in 1945.

The immediate postwar years

Fritz Nallinger had been appointed Chief Engineer in 1940, taking over from Max Sailor. Having been in charge of commercial vehicle development since May 1935, he was already a trusted and highly-experienced member of the Daimler-Benz team, and therefore an ideal candidate for the job.

Like so many manufacturers, Daimler-Benz warmed over some of its prewar designs as part of the rebuilding process, releasing its first postwar car (ignoring utilitarian versions and commercial vehicles) in July 1947 – the bread-and-butter 1.7-litre 170V four-door sedan. By October that year, 1000 had been built, but commercials and repair work dominated the scene in Stuttgart as the transition from military to civilian production took place.

Research and development work recommenced in the middle of 1948. Soon after, the Unimog was unveiled, and car production reached 1000 units a month. Granted, it was still less than half the figure posted in the years leading up to the war, but for Dr Wilhelm Haspel, the company's Chairman, it must have seemed like a definite and most welcome sign of imminent recovery.

Two new 170 series variants (the 170S and 170D) joined the line-up in May 1949, and production continued until 1955, by which time the 180 had been introduced as a

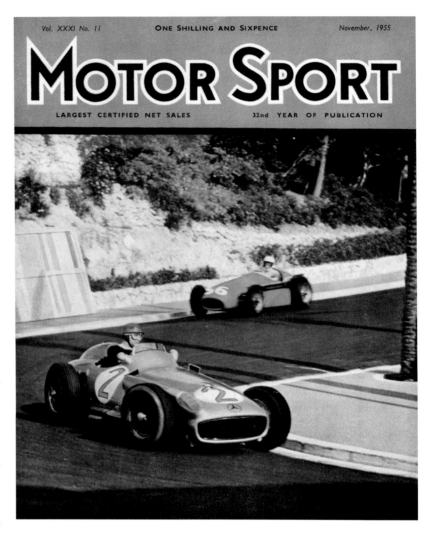

Vol. XXXI No. II   ONE SHILLING AND SIXPENCE   November, 1955

MOTOR SPORT

LARGEST CERTIFIED NET SALES   32nd YEAR OF PUBLICATION

Juan-Manuel Fangio at the wheel of his W196R Grand Prix car – one of the vehicles that helped sustain the 'Silver Arrows' legend established in prewar days.

stablemate. The 170V and 170D were revised in June 1950, receiving, among other things, more powerful engines. Their popularity helped Daimler-Benz breeze towards a landmark figure of 50,000 postwar passenger cars built in October that same year.

Safety considerations were already starting to play an important role in vehicle development at Daimler-Benz. Karl Wilfert (in charge of body development at the Sindelfingen plant) filed a patent for a safety door lock in 1949, and Bela Barenyi

IHR GUTER STERN
AUF ALLEN STRASSEN

Left and above: Thanks to their rugged reliability and high-quality image, Mercedes-Benz cars and trucks were able to forge new markets all over the world. The picture above shows the first 300SL to be transported by air after it arrived at the La Aurora Airport in Guatemala in 1956 – the same year as the advert was released.

came up with the passenger safety cell in 1951. In principle, both of these inventions are still in use to this day.

1951 witnessed the revival of six-cylinder engines with the launch of the 2.2-litre 220 series (W187) and the 3-litre 300 (W186 II) models unveiled in Frankfurt in the latter half of April. The 300 quickly picked up the 'Adenauer' nickname, as the German Chancellor, Konrad Adenauer, was a staunch supporter of the model, and was rarely seen in public without one. The sporting two-door 300S (W188) made its debut later in the year at the Paris Salon.

The 170 series was updated again in 1952, with new models augmenting revised ones, but the debut of the 300SL sports-racer was perhaps the most telling sign that Daimler-Benz was back, its reputation being restored in the showrooms and on the track. A convincing win at Le Mans was followed by a deal with Max Hoffman, which secured a good sales outlet for Mercedes-Benz cars in America. Hoffman also handled Porsche, VW, Alfa Romeo and Jaguar imports for the US, incidentally.

September 1953 marked the arrival of the slab-sided 'Ponton' series, giving the styling cue for a whole new generation of Mercedes-Benz models. It was launched in 1.8-litre four-cylinder guise (W120), but a 2.2-litre six-cylinder version (W180) had joined the line-up by the following spring as a replacement for the W187 model.

On the sporting front, 300SL and 190SL prototypes made their debut at a show in New York in early 1954, in the same year as the W196 Grand Prix car hit the tracks. As expected, it was a winner straight out of the box, and continued to dominate wherever it went in the following season, too. Domination with the 300SLR in the 1955 Mille Miglia was sadly overshadowed by the Le Mans disaster, where many spectators died following a freak accident, and Mercedes withdrew from racing soon after. A second magnificent era in motorsport had come to an end.

In the meantime, Daimler-Benz of North America Inc. was founded in Delaware on 7 April 1955 to handle US imports. With so many new models coming in 1956, such as the 190, 219 and 220S, the timing couldn't have been better. Interestingly, though, in April 1957 (the month after the 300SL Roadster made its debut), a deal was struck with the Curtiss-Wright concern, and the Studebaker-Packard Corporation took on responsibility for the sales of Mercedes-Benz cars and diesel engines in the States. A subsidiary of Studebaker-Packard called Mercedes-Benz Sales Inc. (MBS) was duly formed in August 1958, although this fell by the wayside at the start of 1965, when Mercedes-Benz of North America Inc. (MBNA) took over US operations.

Back in Germany, the passenger car range was overhauled in time for the 1958 Model Year, and during that sales season, power-assisted steering and seatbelts became an option, long before the latter became a legal requirement. Other safety-minded introductions included a new wedge-pin door lock, and a proper crash test programme, which began in earnest at the tail-end of 1959.

Ironically, considering they were bitter rivals in prewar racing, Daimler-Benz acquired a majority interest in Auto Union during 1958. In the following year, plans to take a stake in BMW were thwarted, although the remaining shares in Auto Union were secured at the end of 1959. The company was eventually sold to Volkswagen in 1964, signalling a revival of the Audi name (one of the four firms brought together under the Auto Union marque), later merging it with NSU. Today, Auto Union is ably represented by Audi AG, its cars carrying the same four rings on

Cover of the first brochure released for the thoroughly modern 'Ponton' 190D in 1958. Mercedes-Benz was one of the first manufacturers to promote diesel road cars for public use, and has continued its strong support for CI engines to this day.

their noses as the prewar racers designed by Professor Ferdinand Porsche after he moved from the Mercedes camp. Audi is still owned by the VW group, which has since merged with Porsche. It's a small world in the German car industry!

Meanwhile, September 1958 brought with it a new fuel-injected 220SE (W128) model. Success in the field of long-distance rallying took the place of victories on the track, and success in the showrooms is easy to quantify with annual production averaging around 100,000 units a year by this time, plus around 55,000 commercial vehicles to add to this total. However, the 1959 Frankfurt Show witnessed the dawn of a new era …

2

W123 predecessors

The W123 models had a tough act to follow, with bloodlines incorporating not only the well-received and commercially successful W110 and W111 'Fintail' series, but the ultra-modern '/8' models that followed as well. This chapter takes a brief look at both of these lines to help put the W123 story into perspective ...

The 1959 Frankfurt Show heralded a new era for Daimler-Benz, with the first of the 'Fintail' models lining up alongside a revised four-cylinder 'Ponton' line. When the design work was put in motion during the spring of 1956, it was decided there and then that the 'Fintail' (or 'Heckflosse' in German) series would act as a showcase for the latest Daimler-Benz ideology, with emphasis on safety enhancements and modernity, and hopefully allow the Stuttgart company to penetrate the lucrative US market to a greater extent. At the end of the day, while domestic sales were strong and the brand enjoyed a huge following in all corners of the globe, a larger share of the world's biggest automobile market was certainly going to please those in the accounts department.

The first 'Fintail' saloons

The original 'Fintail' (W111) cars launched in the autumn of 1959 were six-cylinder saloons, replacing the 'Ponton' sixes. Compared to the 'Ponton' machines, the styling was particularly striking, with upright headlights either side of a traditional, rather imposing Mercedes radiator grille, sharper creaselines down the sides and the signature fins at the rear that gave the cars their nickname. In a typically Teutonic way, though, the bold lines managed to remain tasteful and free of gimmicks, allowing the series to appear fresh long after most other finned wonders started to look dated or too contrived.

The men behind the golden age of Mercedes-Benz road cars going over design proposals, including a model of the W113 SL on the left. Design chief Friedrich Geiger is on the left; second from the left is safety supremo Bela Barenyi in conversation with Technical Director Fritz Nallinger, and then we have body engineer Karl Wilfert (with the grey hair and glasses) with Professor Hans Scherenberg sitting next to him (Scherenberg would actually take Nallinger's place at the end of 1965). The gentleman standing on the right-hand side is Professor Werner Breitschwerdt, who would ultimately supercede Scherenberg before going on to a position in the top level of management. Missing from this picture is Chief Development Engineer, Rudolf Uhlenhaut, who gave the cars their distinctive 'feel' on the road.

A 220Sb or 220SEb in the wind tunnel at the Untertürkheim plant, which dates back to 1939. As such, it was one of the first full-size wind tunnels in the industry.

Three four-door saloons were released initially – the 220b, the 220Sb, and the flagship 220SEb. Each was powered by a 2195cc six with a sohc arrangement, with different carburetion on the b and Sb grades giving 95bhp and 110bhp respectively, while the SEb came with fuel-injection and 120bhp. Drive was taken to the rear axle via a traditional manual or 'Hydrak'

transmission – the latter being a special clutch that provided what amounted to a semi-automatic transmission.

The DM 11,500 220b was the base model, while the enhanced trim level on the Sb and SEb was basically the same – the engine was the key difference on these two, with prices ranging from DM 13,250 to DM 14,950. Whichever grade

Mercedes-Benz cars do not reflect the brief "fashion-of-the-moment". They possess a timeless beauty of line. But even more important — Mercedes-Benz are safe. For this is the underlying aim in their design. As the world's oldest automobile manufacturers, Mercedes-Benz have proved how safety can be combined with supreme elegance.

Special chassis stiffeners make the body exceptionally strong. Other outstanding safety features include the unique single-joint swing-axle, with low pivot point and central compensating spring; rubber mounted shock absorbers set close to the wheels; disc brakes, with a duplicated servo-assisted brake system. Daimler-Benz 4-speed automatic transmission is fitted as standard on some of the 14 different models, optional on all other models.

MERCEDES-BENZ

Advertising for the W111 series saloons, this piece being aimed at US servicemen based in Germany, and showing the car's rear suspension. Safety was a key selling point.

Rear three-quarter view of a 220Sb, which readily explains how the 'Fintail' cars picked up their nickname.

event of an accident, and also prevented it from getting jammed. There were also things like a padded steering wheel boss and dashboard fascia, a breakaway rearview mirror, and the option of reasonably-priced seatbelts.

The independent front suspension was made up of unequal-length double-wishbones, a coil spring mounted on the lower arm, and a telescopic shock absorber placed close to the road wheel. At the back, there was a familiar swing-axle arrangement, complete with a transverse compensator spring, with the IRS made up of trailing arms, plus coil springs on one side of the axle line, and telescopic shocks on the other. The tried-and-trusted recirculating ball steering set-up was called out for duty once more, with 'Al-Fin' drums providing the braking at all four corners (with a brake servo on the more powerful machines), and crossply tyres as standard fare.

Model proliferation

Although the three original 'Fintail' lines entered the 1961 season virtually unchanged, they were joined by a number of variants during the spring of that year. First up was the W111 220SEb Coupé, officially launched at the 1961 Geneva Show. This was a luxury four-seater GT built on the same floorpan as the saloons,

was chosen, however, passengers were treated to much more interior space compared to users of the 'Ponton' models, superb ergonomics, and one of the safest environments on the road. Safety features included a stiff passenger cell with innovative deformation 'crumple zones' at the front and rear (something we take for granted now, but leading-edge technology back then), special door locks that stopped the door flying open in the but with all the outer panels revised to make the car lower and wider – both visually and physically.

Most will agree that the styling of the two-door model was majestic, with clean lines, an attractive roof and glasshouse shape; the fins becoming less obvious around the back. The Coupé also had the distinction of being the first Mercedes-Benz to adopt disc brakes, a month before the 300SL gained them. The Coupé had them at the front only, whereas the SL had them on all four wheels. Notwithstanding, as soon as sales started, a four-speed automatic transmission became available, adding DM 1400 to the car's DM 23,500 list price, and PAS was made an option for all 'Fintail' models a couple of months later.

Visitors to the 1961 Frankfurt Show were treated to the public debut of the W111 220SEb Cabriolet, the W110 190c and 190Dc models, and the high-class W112 300SE. The DM 25,500 Cabriolet was basically a drophead version of the 220SEb Coupé, although its flagship status was confirmed by an automatic transmission, air suspension, power steering, and disc brakes coming as standard.

A contemporary colour shot of the 220SEb Coupé.

An early 190c photographed in Africa. Mercedes vehicles were always popular in these out-of-the-way places, where reliability was of paramount importance.

U 13797

The four-cylinder 190s replaced the last of the 'Ponton' machines. These W110 models had a revised front-end that allowed the car to be shorter without encroaching on interior space, and were readily identified by their simple headlight arrangement. The DM 9950 190c was powered by a 1897cc four developing 80bhp, while the 190Dc added a diesel variant – a 1988cc four that gave 55bhp and greater frugality for a DM 500 premium. Both came with a 4MT gearbox only, although both four-cylinder models could also be bought in special purpose chassis guise to allow coachbuilders to work their handicraft. A few of the minor trim changes applied to the 190s were carried over to the 220b at the same time, while the braking system was upgraded on the 220Sb and 220SEb lines.

The other model launched at this time was the DM 24,150 3-litre 300SE saloon. This was powered by a lightened version of the M189 straight-six, with an alloy block and fuel-injection.

The 2996cc unit gave 160bhp DIN, and was hooked up to an automatic transmission only. As well as lashings of chrome and enhanced interior fixtures and fittings, air suspension, PAS, disc brakes all-round, and a limited-slip differential were classed as standard items.

The DM 32,750 300SE Coupé and DM 34,750 300SE Cabriolet were launched at the 1962 Geneva Show, and disc brakes became the norm on the 220Sb and 220SEb saloons a month later, in April. The last of the 300SE variants was released a year later – the lwb 300SE Lang, which could be bought with a manual gearbox as an option. As it happens, the automatic transmission had become available on the 190c, 220b and 220Sb by this time, too, with 190Dc drivers eventually getting the option in July 1963.

The SL range was also brought up to date during 1963, when the 230SL (W113) replaced the 190SL and 300SL, bridging the

One of the first 300SE saloons pictured at Stuttgart Airport. Note the extra chromework that helped distinguish the 3-litre models from the regular line.

Above and right: The 'Fintail' models were actually quite successful in motorsport, doing well in the likes of the Monte Carlo Rally (this is the 1963 edition, when Evy Rosqvist and Ursula Wirth won the Ladies Prize), and even events like the Spa 24-hour Race – the poster commemorating the outright victory scored by the 300SE in 1964.

Mercedes-Benz Sieg

Mercedes-Benz 300 SE gewinnt
24-Stunden-Rennen von Francorchamps

In diesem spannenden und harten Tourenwagenrennen errangen Robert Crevits/Georges Gosselin mit einer Durchschnitts-geschwindigkeit von 164,875 km/h – 281 Runden und einer Runde Vorsprung den ersten Platz im Gesamtklassement.

Eugen Böhringer auf Mercedes-Benz 300 SE fuhr mit 177,296 km/h die schnellste Runde.

Von 55 gestarteten Wagen konnten nur 24 gewertet werden.

The 300SE Coupé from around 1964, as the mirror has been moved to the door, but the wheels have yet to be changed.

gap between the two in many ways, but the modern styling was another sign that the Mercedes-Benz brand had moved on a generation. Similar lines were chosen for the upmarket 1964 V8-engined 600 – a stately vehicle available as a 5/6-seater or 7/8-seater on an extended wheelbase.

All 'Fintail' cars gained disc brakes with a dual-circuit system and a brake servo in time for the 1964 season, and the side mirrors were moved from the front wings to the doors. There were also new foglights for the four-cylinder models, and different rear combination lights for the W110 cars and the 220b. A little

A W108 series car on test at Untertürkheim, with a W110 'Fintail' model in the background.

The 300SEL 6.3 creating a stir at the 1968 Geneva Show.

while later, the 300SE models gained an extra ten horses under the bonnet, and PAS became available on the 190s in May 1964. Bigger changes were around the corner, though …

The 1965 Frankfurt Show

Things moved forward again in September 1965, when the W108 and W109 models replaced the majority of the 'Fintail' six-cylinder saloons, although the two-door models and four-cylinder W110 line continued for a while longer, duly joined by the 250SL before augmenting the 280SL and a new range of '/8' machines that took the place of the 'Fintail' fours at the start of 1968.

The W108 and lwb W109 were closer to S-Class predecessors than E-Class models, in fact, filling the gap created by the loss of the W112 'Fintail' models at the top-end of the luxury saloon market until the W116 models came

online at the end of 1972. The first cars of the line included the 250S, 250SE, 300SE and 300SEL, with modern styling that reflected the past, yet still managed to point towards the future. By the start of 1968, the 250SE and 300SE had been replaced by the 2778cc 280S and 280SE, the engine in the 300SEL changed to a smaller unit, and the mighty 300SEL 6.3 had been introduced.

Before moving on to the '/8' series, it's worth a couple of paragraphs to round off the 'Fintail' era, as things get extremely confusing if one jumps ahead too quickly. The latest W110 models inherited new foglights with integral indicator units, C-post vents, a new rear combination lamp design, and a revised interior, although the main changes were mechanical. The 190c saloon became the DM 10,800 200 after adopting a new 95bhp 1988cc powerplant; the diesel version became the DM 11,300 200D, and the DM 11,700 230 was an oddball newcomer – a 2306cc six in the bodyshell meant for the four-

cylinder car. As such, this latter machine carried a W110 chassis code, although one final W111 model was released at the same time, which was the DM 13,750 230S, with a 120bhp version of the latest straight-six. The 230S featured the upright headlights of its W111 predecessors, so this one was easy to spot, even if it was difficult to understand its late inclusion in the line-up when the '/8' machines were grabbing the limelight. Again, special purpose chassis versions were made available, including diesel and long-wheelbase variants, and there was even an off-the-peg 'Universal' estate made – offered as a production vehicle through Mercedes dealers from August 1966 onwards.

At the same time as all this was happening, the two-door W111s gained a fresh 2496cc engine, giving birth to the 250SE Coupé and 250SE Cabriolet. After getting the new brakes and wheels from the 250s, the 300SE Coupé and 300SE Cabriolet were carried over, by the way, with only the two 3-litre saloons falling by the wayside.

By the spring of 1967, a lwb seven-/eight-seater saloon had been marketed on the 200D platform, and in July, a number of fresh safety measures were adopted, including a safety steering column that telescoped in the event of an accident. The two-door cars also gained three-point safety belts. However, production on all four of the two-door models and the 230S ended in December 1967, with that of the W110 cars coming to an end in the following month.

Even this wasn't quite the end of the story, though, for a new 280SE Coupé and 280SE Cabriolet were listed from January 1968. Featuring a new rear suspension, these were powered by a 2778cc M130 six rated at 160bhp, and made their debut priced at DM 26,510 and DM 28,545, respectively. These were joined by 3499cc V8-engined variants at the 1969 Frankfurt Show – the

DM 30,636 280SE 3.5 Coupé and the DM 34,132 280SE 3.5 Cabriolet, which were launched alongside the W109 300SEL 3.5 saloon and the Wankel-engined C111. This magnificent creation was perhaps too far ahead of its time, although it's a shame that more wasn't done with the rotary engine – after a few more C111 prototypes, as with so many companies that had paid NSU for patent rights, the RE adventure came to an end.

The W111 V8 machines had a lower, wider front grille, which was duly adopted by their six-cylinder stablemates, although the last of the 'Fintail' models were finally built in the middle of 1971. It is worth noting at this stage that 280SE

Production at the Sindelfingen plant in 1967, with the lines being shared by the new '/8' series cars, W110 models, and the odd W111 230S.

Some of the last W108 and W109 models on the line at Sindelfingen, with a very early R107 roadster pushing in. While the tiny tailfins on the W108 were an evolution of those found on the two-door 'Fintail' models, the modern styling of the SL would provide the inspiration for the forthcoming W123 series.

A 'Fintail' swansong in the form of the V8-engined 280SE 3.5 Coupé and Cabriolet.

3.5 and 280SEL 3.5 models extended the W108/W109 series in February 1971, just before the R107 SL was launched. Introduced in April, the two-seater V8 roadster was joined by a slightly longer tin-top version (the C107, or SLC) at the end of the year. There were also 4.5-litre versions of the big saloons produced, mainly for the American market, although production of the W108 and W109 machines came to an end with the introduction of the W116 S-Class, which duly took a bow at the 1972 Paris Salon. The '/8' range continued to evolve, however ...

The '/8' Series
The first of the W114 and W115 '/8' models was launched alongside the W108 280S and 280SE, as well as the W113 280SL, at a special event at Hockenheim in the early part of January 1968, hence the '/8' (or 'Stroke Eight') reference. These 'New Generation' cars were a thoroughly modern interpretation of traditional Mercedes thinking, overseen by Dr Hans Scherenberg,

A useful picture, as it shows the '/8' model's rear-end styling as well as the car's cavernous boot.

One of the new '/8' models. The 200, 200D, 220, 220D and 230 all look similar, with only the 250 having a unique bumper.

Der älteste Automobilherstel-
ler der Welt bietet Ihnen die
neue Mercedes-Benz Generation: Limousinen verschiedener
Klassen, einschließlich Diesel-
Modellen, Coupés, Cabriolets
und Sportwagen. Es gibt größere, aufwendigere und teurere
Wagen auf der Welt. Aber
wahrscheinlich keine besseren.

The world's oldest automobile
maker offers the new Mercedes-
Benz Generation: limousines,
sedans, coupes, sports cars and
Diesel economy cars. There are
larger and more overbearing
and costlier cars in the world.
But there are prob-
ably none better.
Mercedes-Benz

Gesamtprogramm:
200 D, 220 D, 200, 220, 230, 250, 250 S, 280 S, 280 SE, 280 SL,
300 SEL, 300 SEL 6.3, 600.

Einladung zur Probefahrt!
Es gibt nun einmal Unterschiede in Komfort
und Straßenlage. Erfahren Sie, wie groß
der Unterschied sein kann.

Mercedes-Benz   Ihr guter Stern auf allen Straßen

Walter Schmidt Vertreter der Daimler-Benz AG
24 Lübeck · Fackenburger Allee 66 · Telefon 42441/44

Left and above: Advertising from 1968, showing the 250/8
with its twin bumper blades, and the W108 280S, which was
introduced at the same time as the W114 model. The second
piece shows the W114/W115 interior.

who took over the responsibility for product development
following the retirement of Professor Fritz Nallinger at the end
of 1965.

Apart from the styling, which was a slightly sharper
interpretation of the W108 body, with simpler upright headlight

housings, less rounded flanks, and larger taillights around the back, the key component in the new model was the so-called diagonal swing-axle. This was the first time Daimler-Benz had employed a semi-trailing rear suspension, made up of a centre boomerang-shaped cradle that had a fabricated wishbone cum wheel carrier attached to it at both sides, which duly located the coil spring with a shock absorber down its centre; the independent front suspension was basically a double-wishbone set-up, with a coil spring and a separate telescopic shock absorber mounted close to the wheel. Disc brakes were fitted all-round, with recirculating ball steering, and the possibility of radial tyres.

The four-cylinder W115 line-up included the DM 11,495 200, DM 11,990 200D and 220, and the DM 12,485 220D. All were powered by sohc units with carburettors, with the 1988cc diesel being the weakest of the bunch, rated at 55bhp, and the 2197cc petrol engine the strongest, developing a healthy 105bhp. As for the six-cylinder W114 models, there was the DM 13,145 230 and DM 14,630 250, the latter readily identified by being the only model in the '/8' range to feature a twin bumper blade arrangement up front. These were powered by an engine much the same as the four-cylinder units but with two extra pots, giving 120bhp in the case of the 2292cc lump, and 130bhp on the 2496cc motor. A four-speed manual gearbox was the norm on all cars, with automatic transmission (4AT on the fours, and 5AT on the sixes) available as an option.

As 1968 continued, an attractive W114 coupé broke cover, which eventually went into production during the following year. The first cars were the 250C and 250CE, and combined with the existing saloons, the numerous special purpose chassis versions for coachbuilders (five in all, available in standard- and long-wheelbase form), and the 220D and 230 eight-seater lwb models that were launched at the end of 1969, the range was both extensive and varied. One final model came in the form of the US market 250, for this was powered by a sohc 2778cc M130 unit from mid-1970 onwards.

Incidentally, Hermann J Abs resigned as Chairman of the Daimler-Benz AG Supervisory Board in 1970, handing the reins to Franz Heinrich Ulrich. A few months later, Dr Joachim Zahn was made Chairman of the Board of Management, while the Hanomag truck concern became a wholly-owned subsidiary of

An early W114 coupé.

A striking angle from which to view the 280CE. Note the rear bumper and twin exhaust pipes.

The 2.8-litre W114s were easy to recognize, as they were the only cars to have both the heavier front bumper arrangement and a full-length rear bumper blade. The 280 was introduced at DM 18,980, while the fuel-injected model commanded DM 20,535.

Stylish publicity shot of a face-lifted W114 or W115 model, with its new front grille, revised door mirror design, and front number plate moved onto the bumper blade instead of underneath it.

the Stuttgart giant (the tractor side of the business was separated and sold to Massey Ferguson).

Not long after, in April 1972, a new batch of W114 models joined the range, giving Mercedes-Benz a particularly sporting ambience in time to complement the luxury W116 S-Class. These were powered by M110 2746cc dohc sixes with the carbureted 160bhp 280 and 280C being joined by the fuel-injected 185bhp 280E and 280CE. At the same time, the European 250 also received the 130bhp 2778cc sohc engine, as per American-spec vehicles.

To improve safety, the four-spoke steering wheel found on the S-Class models was adopted in March 1973, along with head restraints and automatic seatbelts. However, production of the original '/8' series came to an end in August, as the Sindelfingen factory began preparing itself for a revised W114/ W115 range.

A 'Stroke Eight' overhaul

The 1973 Frankfurt Show played host to a face-lifted W114 and W115 line-up. It took a real enthusiast to spot the differences, but they were there alright. Most of the modifications were aimed at improving safety, such as new door mirrors with adjustment possible from inside the car, new A-post trims to help keep the side windows clear, and a heavier trim over the top of the rear window to help it stay cleaner for longer. There was also a new rear combination light design that was ultimately carried over to the W123 models in principle, its strong ribs helping to reduce road dirt build-up. Other changes included a lower, wider front grille, one-piece front side windows, a revised boot plinth, and loss of the double bumper blade arrangement on the more expensive models, although the 280s continued to sport their own, unique rear bumper.

On the mechanical front, the 220 was dropped when the old engine was replaced by an M115 2307cc unit, thus giving birth to the 230.4 model (the 230.6 designation was duly adopted on

Contemporary shot of the imposing head office in the Untertürkheim district of Stuttgart.

Detail shot of the latest rear combination light design, seen here on a 240D. All cars except the 2.8-litre models shared this style of rear bumper, by the way.

the old six-cylinder 230 to avoid confusion). There was also a new 240D with a 65bhp 2404cc four under the bonnet, which augmented the saloon line-up, but took the place of the 220D in the eight-seater and chassis-only line-up. The 80bhp 240D 3.0 was the final addition (classed as a W115 model), arriving in July 1974 to become the world's first five-cylinder diesel-engined car.

In the background, Mercedes-Benz UK Ltd was formed as 1974 dawned, the same year in which the SL line gained a six-cylinder engine option, while 1975 saw the launch of the 450SEL 6.9 – a true wolf in sheep's clothing. With a workforce of roughly 150,000 at this time, annual production during 1975 stood at 350,098 cars and 229,302 trucks.

The '/8' model's replacement was unveiled to the press in January 1976, although the line continued for a little while longer, running alongside its successor until the tail-end of 1976. The bigger-engined models and coupés were the first to go, disappearing in the summer, but some grades continued into December. By the time the final W114/W115 series car had been built, almost two-million examples had found new homes all across the globe. The W123 certainly had a hard act to follow ...

Interior of the 280E following its face-lift.

34

A 280CE with the optional alloy wheels that were the epitome of the era. As it happens, it was probably the coupé that benefited the most from the styling updates, looking altogether better balanced than the early versions.

American advertising from the summer of 1975 for the S-Class model. It's fair to say that the W116 was as much a predecessor of the W123 as the smaller line of cars it would replace. One look at the styling and chassis components will quickly tell you that …

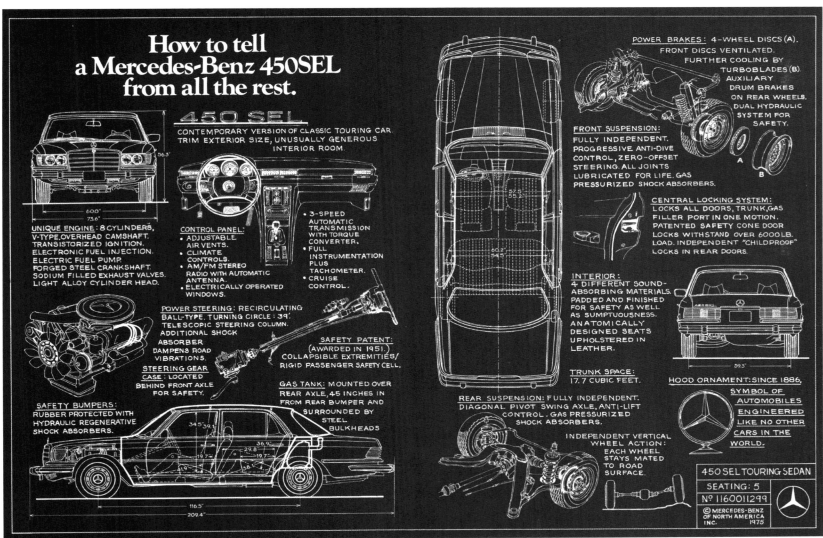

3

Birth of the W123 series

As one will have gathered from reading the last chapter, the replacement for the 'Stroke Eight' models had a hard act to follow – the mid-size line had been an unprecedented success for Daimler-Benz, firstly thanks to the 'Fintail' range, and then the cars that followed. They were loved by the press and public alike, but times were changing across the globe, with the United States in particular becoming more vocal on safety and emission regulations, and the Stuttgart company needed to move with them …

The hardest part in the design of any car is achieving a balance between innovation and function. Given a free hand, most stylists would like to design a machine that set the world alight with modernity and lines that looked superb because they didn't have to allow for practical issues. In the real world, they are given the task of moving a vehicle range forward in a way that builds on heritage (helping keep the value of older cars high), and, due to the slow pace of Daimler-Benz model changes, retain its fresh looks for the best part of a decade, which tends to eliminate fashionable trends that tend to date a car all too quickly. So, especially in the case of a mass-production saloon, the best we can hope for is a formula that gives us something with timeless elegance, along with new levels of safety, comfort and practicality.

Preliminary design work on the W123 series began not long after the launch of the 'Stroke Eight' range, and a good deal of progress had already been made on the new car's styling by 1969. While shades of the forthcoming W116 S-Class were clearly visible in many designs, early proposals showed a huge amount of variation, including a number of fastbacks (one looked much like the Tatra T613) and even a few sketches with unusual reverse-rake rooflines resembling the one used on the Citroën Ami. However, it's fair to say that strong, boxy shapes dominated, with the styling of the favourite during the initial stages leaning towards that of the UK-made Ford Zephyr and Zodiac Mark IV

models from the mid-1960s, showing a remarkable likeness around the tail, but with rectangular headlights up front. It was the way German design was going at the time, with BMW, Audi, Ford-Werke (Ford Europe after the merger with the UK operation) and Opel all adopting strong three-box shapes, while in other parts of Europe, the likes of Fiat, Peugeot and Volvo continued the trend, which by now had firmly established itself in the States, too.

By the summer of 1970, under the watchful gaze of Chief Designer Friedrich Geiger, the majority of styling features were in place on certain clay models, with only detail items like light units and the final touches to the radiator grille needing further refinement. There were still many options on the table, though, with full-size styling bucks being made of the Ami-inspired car (the rear cowl that extended the roofline having actually been a dominant feature on a number of Geiger's more adventurous proposals from the past), as well as a few designs that were obviously aimed at pleasing customers on the other side of the Atlantic to Europe.

With the decision having been made to closely follow the W116 concept by the time 1971 came around, a number of mock-ups were presented to the Board of Management along with the W123's predecessors, contemporary Mercedes models, and a number of vehicles in the same market sector from rival manufacturers. The three white prototypes were already

Head of styling, Friedrich Geiger (in the white coat), seen here in the early 1960s with Karl Wilfert (head of bodywork development until Guntram Huber took his place in 1973) on the left, and Fritz Nallinger, Hans Scherenberg's predecessor as the man with overall responsibility for vehicle and engine development.

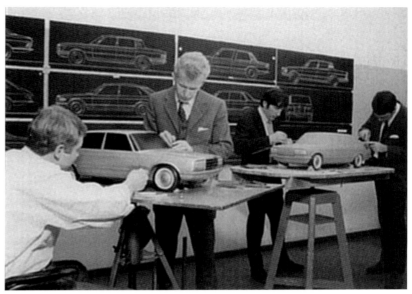

A busy design studio, pictured in 1969.

One of the many one-fifth scale models produced, along with a cutaway version used to study structural alternatives. These type of models were mainly used to refine production techniques before the heavy investment required for tooling began.

remarkably close to the production design, with two of them featuring the headlights found on showroom models (although the rectangular version was shallower at this stage), and one with a pair of smaller circular lights instead of a larger outside unit combined with a smaller inner one. The prototype with the rectangular headlights had rear lights close to those of the production car, but shorter (like those of the late '/8' models) and combined with a filler piece that visually reduced the bulk underneath the bootlid, while the other two cars had huge units, the size of those found on the W116 S-Class but featuring a pair

A styling buck dated September 1970. This was an era when modern rear light units were really starting to evolve.

January 1973, and the window shapes have been finalized on Model 1. The rear combination lamps are close to production style, too, except for their size and positioning; the boards in the background show the subtle differences being looked into for the headlight and indicator arrangement up front as well.

A 1971 design clinic, with three W123 mock-ups flanked by current and forthcoming Mercedes models, and a selection of rivals on the opposite side.

A full-size clay (this one marked up as Model 6) photographed in June 1971. Note the dip in the side window graphics – a theme later seen in the coupé – and the round rear lights.

of round, chrome-framed inserts on each side. Other details for consideration included window trims, waistline garnish pieces, bumper finish lines, and so on, but they were indeed detail changes that were being reviewed rather than fundamental design features.

The bickering over tiny details continued into the summer of 1973, confirming that the Board was in no hurry to replace the '/8' line, and an initial production start date of autumn 1974 came and went, as did the spring 1975 one. Finally, with the very latest robots having been installed at Sindelfingen to look

after almost all of the body welds (thus improving quality and productivity, enabling the old line workers to concentrate on hand-finishing and other skilled tasks), pilot production began in late-July 1975, with the first showroom models rolling off the line at the end of the year.

A new body

The W123's unit construction body represented a masterful blend of S-Class styling features and a touch of individuality to provide a suitable distance between the mid-level range and the flagship models. Followers of Mercedes-Benz lore can see the evolutionary steps that brought the car about, with the lower, wider grille introduced on the first of the V8 cars showing the way forward, and the headlights inspired by the 107 series SL/SLC and the contemporary W116 luxury saloons. Whereas the '/8' had always kept an eye firmly on the past, with a number of 'Fintail' styling cues carried over, the W123 was a thoroughly modern machine.

Starting with the grille, as the centrepiece of any Mercedes front-end, it looked a lot less formal than that of the '/8' cars – aping that of the new S-Class saloons, it was a fair bit lower and a fraction narrower than the one found on the W114/W115 cars, and with a narrower top edge that still gave the onlooker a means of instant identification, but in a far more subtle manner than before. Interestingly, though, while the S-Class retained the classic cheese-cutter grille inserts found on the older cars, the W123s adopted a series of small horizontal slats – something that was duly continued as a feature on future entry-level and E-Class machines. As always, the top section of the grille was adorned by a star and laurels badge set below a three-pointed star, the latter being ball-jointed to allow it to move if hit.

Just before full-scale production began, a subtle change was made to the radiator grille – this only affected the first couple of hundred 280s; the design was finalized by the time the majority of models started being built, and is difficult to spot anyway. The

39

The front face of the new W123 series, with that used on the European 280 and 280E seen on the left, and less expensive grades on the right. The US-spec light looked similar to those used on the right-hand car at first glance, but used sealed beam units within the same housing.

The bumper arrangement on the majority of cars, with a rubber dressing piece on the trailing edge.

same is true of a change made a few days later, allowing the bootlid to close with less force.

Moving to the side of the grille, the rectangular headlights now sat horizontally rather than vertically, butting up to the radiator grille on the one side and providing a flush mounting surface for the separate indicator units on their outer edge. Three basic types of headlights were produced – one with a pair of round lights contained in the glass housing, complete with decorative slats to continue the theme of the grille (fitted to the majority of cars); a version for the top ROW models with a squared-off halogen main light unit to match the halogen foglight, again with slats along the bottom edge to fill the same amount of space as the regular light unit, and a US version with round lights but no glass cover. There were also a few market-specific light units produced for places like France, which demanded yellow lenses for the foglights, for instance, but it's still safe to say there were three main types.

The indicator units were shaped in such a way as to do away with the need for side markers. They were chunky enough to be visible from the front, and curved around the side to such an extent that separate markers were no longer required in places like America. A small piece of flat sheet-metal was added to bridge the gap below the headlight and above the bumper blade, and this provided a perfect mounting point for the optional headlight wipers. As a result, the latter items were a lot better integrated than they had been on the '/8' cars.

On the '/8' models, some had had a single bumper blade, while others had carried twin bumpers in the early days to continue a tradition established on the more expensive 'Fintail' cars. For the W123, all cars had a single chrome bumper blade with a space for the number plate in the centre and rubber inserts that wrapped around the wing edges on the 280s. For other cars, there was a minor difference on the bumper that helps distinguish lesser models, and that is the rubber corner dressing piece rather than an extension of the chrome blade – this bridged the gap between ROW- and US-spec cars, the latter needing a heftier bumper arrangement in order to meet the questionable Federal regulations in place at the time. Underneath this was a large intake, with the painted sheet metal below shaped to follow its profile. Combined with a tiny black chin spoiler set back a touch, and hardly visible most of

This pre-production model shows the all-chrome front bumper used on the 280 and 280E grades. The rubbing strip down the centre of the blade was the same for all cars, however.

the time, this feature was a thoroughly modern piece of design that showed the generation gap between the W123s and the older '/8' machines.

Moving further back, the rear-hinged bonnet (which could actually open at a regular 45 degree or 90 degree angle by manipulating the hinges) featured a power bulge like that of its predecessors, albeit with the trailing edges being kept more central, and the lower parts of the bonnet blending smoothly with the wings – there was no longer a dip to highlight the headlight pods. As before, the screen washer nozzles were kept on the bonnet rather than the bulkhead, which helped keep the washer fluid warm during winter months. Incidentally, although a few early pictures show chrome nozzles, they were black on showroom models.

On the bulkhead, the old chrome-plated clap-hands windscreen wipers were replaced by wipers following a more

The novel bonnet, with two-position opening to aid production, but a feature that was also useful during servicing.

conventional pattern mounted on offset pivots, covering some 20 per cent more of the screen than before and finished in matt black to reduce glare. There was also a more rounded line at the base of the windscreen, helping to visually reduce the acres of metal used for the bonnet, with the air vent below becoming separated into a pair of vents that were pushed outwards to follow the bonnet line; the vent grilles were black on most cars, and chrome on the 2.8-litre models.

Side views of the new saloon in left-hand drive guise, with the fuel filler door located on the offside rear wing. For the record, the saloon had a drag coefficient figure of Cd 0.42.

However, while it's fair to say the latest car looked completely new below the waistline, the front view beyond the bulkhead was strikingly similar except for a few details. The angle of lean on the front pillars was basically carried over, along with the roof profile, but there was a new A-post trim that kept rain and dirt off the side windows, and directed water above them via revised rain channels; the pillars were also kept as thin as possible to improve vision, and thus improve safety. Finally, the rather hefty but stylish door mirrors were the same as those fitted to the last of the '/8' models, the design being shared with the contemporary S-Class vehicle line.

Viewed from the side, the old and the new machines were remarkably similar. The elegant curve at the top edge of the front wing was still there, but the indicator lights made an interesting feature to break up the panel, and the area below the bumper was much more aggressive, although practical thinking and improved fuel efficiency via enhanced aerodynamics were the priority rather than a deliberate move towards macho styling. Below the full length black and chrome rubbing strip (a carry-over feature), the wheelarch profile was more rounded than before, and a creasline was added that ran from the trailing edge of the front wheelarch to the top of the rear bumper blade, breaking up the expanse of metal and giving the panelwork extra strength at the same time. Another black and chrome strip dressed the sill area just below the doors, aping the older cars, although the metalwork below this was blacked out between the front and rear wheels to visually reduce the vehicle's height, at least on lighter-coloured cars. A nice touch was making the doors overlap the sill, thus keeping the outer edge of the rocker area clean so as not to soil clothing when people got into or out of the car.

In keeping with the rest of the design, the leading edge on the doors was more rounded than before, as were the window graphics beyond the new A-post trim at the top edge. However, apart from the new door handles (a modern interpretation of those fitted to the SL at the time) and the lack of a swivelling quarter-vent on the front window (deleted on the 'Stroke Eight' saloons for the 1974 season anyway), the shapes and chrome trim arrangement was very similar to that found on the '/8' cars. The same could be said of the back door, which was even closer to the earlier design, although the C-post trim that led off it was revised to improve interior ventilation, and the finishing piece at the base of the C-pillar was far more elegant than that fitted to the earlier cars. In fact, the latter trim section was a functional part, hiding a joint that allowed easy replacement of the rear wing, thus reducing accident repair costs – something the designers had been asked to bear in mind from the outset.

Moving further back, the top of the rear window was given a softer profile, and the wheelarch shape was rounder than before, albeit retaining the signature swoop on the trailing edge that could be traced back to the 'Fintail' era. The rear bumpers were short on all cars, with the 280s all-chrome to match those up front, and rubber corner pieces for other grades, while the rear light units, protected by their own rubber (or rubber and chrome) trim at the base, extended further than the older lights to do away with the need for side markers on US-bound cars. The lowermost parts, peeking out from beneath the valance underneath the bumpers were blacked out, as per the '/8' machines, but something totally new was a fuel filler door on the offside rear wing instead of to the right of the rear number plate; the radio aerial was fitted on the nearside rear wing, incidentally, which signalled another move, as it had previously been positioned on the front offside wing. Finally, the basic wheel trims were much the same as those found on the '/8' series.

Size comparisons

A quick reference guide to the evolution of the mid-range line, from the W111 'Fintail' models through to the W123 series, taking a look at the early W114/W115 '/8' line along the way:

	W111	W115	W123
Wheelbase	2750mm (108.2in)	2750mm (108.2in)	2795mm (110.0in)
Length	4875mm (191.9in)	4680mm (184.3in)	4725mm (186.0in)
Height	1510mm (59.4in)	1440mm (56.7in)	1438mm (56.6in)
Width	1795mm (70.7in)	1770mm (69.7in)	1786mm (70.3in)
Track (F)	1470mm (57.9in)	1444mm (56.8in)	1488mm (58.6in)
Track (R)	1485mm (58.5in)	1440mm (56.7in)	1446mm (56.9in)

Rear view of an early 300D saloon, with the rubber corner pieces used on the bumper of all cars except the 280 and 280E.

Around the back, the most striking feature was the heavily-ribbed rear combination light unit design, which was an evolution of the one found on the '/8' models from the 1974 MY onwards, and featured an integral rear foglight. The ribbing helped keep the lights cleaner for longer, while the rubber (or rubber and chrome) insert fitted beneath offered them protection from low-speed parking knocks; they were also protected at the top by the waist-level trim that curved around the rear wings and was duly continued across the lower edge of the bootlid, as per the '/8' models.

It was hard to spot the different bumper designs when looking at the car from directly behind, but those fitted to the 280s did stand a touch prouder of the body compared with those that had the rubber corner pieces. In any case, both came with a heavy rubber insert to match that used up front, and all cars had a slightly softer look to the rear window graphics compared to the previous saloons.

The general look aped that of the contemporary S-Class, with a narrow piece of bodywork above the bumper, and a narrow rear valance finished in body colour, hiding most of the exhaust pipe, which was always positioned on the nearside.

Tail of one of the pre-production 2.8-litre cars. Note the all-chrome bumper, matching the one up front, and the twin exhaust pipes. The warning triangle would remain the same during the 123 series run, incidentally, although a folding one was employed on the estates.

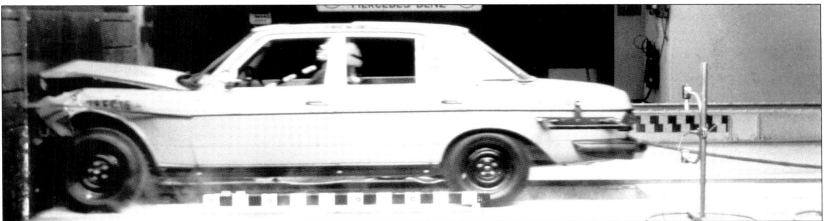

Safety was of paramount importance to those in charge at Daimler-Benz. Even after the W123 was launched, research continued to find ways in which the car could be improved. This particular crash test took place in 1978.

Even the minute kick in the rear wings (which was surely added in reverence of the 'Fintail' cars) and badging was similar, with the model designation on the left and a large three-pointed star in the centre of the bootlid. However, the boot plinth, which was used on both the W114/W115 and W116 cars, was done away with, and the trunk release button (placed directly underneath the star as per the S-Class rather than on the bootlid trim, as had been the case on the '/8' models) was given a less ornate mount than that found on the more expensive machines.

When design work began on the W123 series, one of the key points in the brief was to make the car safer than its immediate predecessors, and naturally conform to all current and any known forthcoming regulations with ease. Using a lot of the valuable R&D work that had gone into the R107 and W116 models, safety supremo Bela Barenyi (christened the father of passive safety, with around 2500 patents to his name) saw to it that the passenger safety cell was stiffer than ever before, while the front and rear crumple zones were allowed to deform at a rate that best absorbed and dispersed energy from an accident, be it frontal or offset. At the same time, the roof structure was made stronger, and in conjunction with the stiffer sills, door pillars and special door locks, this helped protect passengers in a

side-impact or roll-over situation. Even things like the new spare wheel position had been planned beforehand, keeping it as low as possible underneath the boot floor to limit damage in a rear-end shunt and reduce the car's centre of gravity, while the fuel tank (65 litres/14.3 Imperial or 17.2 US gallons on most cars, but 80 litres/17.6 Imperial or 21.1 US gallons on the 2.8-litre machines) was located directly above the rear axle, using the strength of the axle itself in order to protect the tank as much as possible from all directions.

Quality and longevity were other considerations. The build quality angle was looked after by mechanized production techniques, with robots bringing a level of consistency to the equation that even the finest craftsmen in Germany would have found difficult to duplicate, and they certainly couldn't compete with R2D2's friends on things like speed and stamina. Hand-finishing was kept to an absolute minimum, again enhancing overall fit and finish, as well as productivity through the accompanying reduction in manufacturing time.

As for longevity, the steel monocoque shell was given a multi-stage protection plan to inhibit rust – rust being one of the few complaints that could be directed at the '/8' series. Firstly, after thorough cleaning, the body was coated in zinc phosphate, which provides a perfect key for primer, then given an electrophoretic dip, two primer coats of paint, and finally the coloured top coats. The body was then duly given further long-term protection via the application of underseal and a light petroleum-based preservative underneath the car, and a special wax being pumped into cavities that were deemed to be at risk from the dreaded tin-worm. Looking at cars today, it's fair to say that the expense and attention to detail paid off, as rusty W123 models are quite rare compared to contemporary saloons from other makers.

Inside story

The basic layout for the W116-inspired interior was already in place by 1970, with safety, improved ergonomics and the need for greater interior space shaping the format rather than 'Olde Worlde' charm. Although Daimler-Benz had always been at the forefront of safety thought and technology, thanks to Barenyi, a lot of detail work had been done to satisfy Federal regulations during the late-1960s, when the growing significance of the US market made it too important to ignore, and all of the ideas

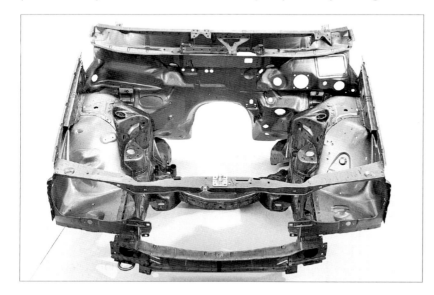

Build quality was enhanced via the use of robots for welding the bodyshell, ensuring accuracy and consistency during the spot-welding process.

Driver controls of a very early W123 saloon. On rhd cars, the lighting switch, indicator stalk, and ignition barrel positions were reversed.

The fascia of a car without wood trim, which is the majority of W123s in reality. Note the original-style cloth upholstery.

and clock adjuster in the same strip. Each gauge was individual, with various markings and calibrations teamed up to suit various markets, while the clear plastic cover in the warning bank section could also be changed with ease to suit the car's options and local regulations. Whatever the market, though, the buyer was guaranteed excellent legibility in the instruments.

The top roll featured four directional eyeball vents, with two in the centre (with their own air volume control slider underneath), and two at each end that were twisted one way or the other to control airflow, and helped keep the side windows clear when needed. Beyond these outer air vents were the speaker grilles, with a full-width screen vent sitting between them. Separating the black top roll from the lower section was a horizontal insert that was either a soft perforated vinyl (in black) or wood-effect section depending on the grade – generally speaking, the 2.8-litre cars were the only ones to benefit from the Zebrano trim pieces.

Underneath this was another moulded black section that provided a mounting plinth for the parking brake release knob (or pistol-grip handbrake mechanism on rhd cars) and the superb rotary light switch on one side of the steering column, and – on petrol cars – the ignition barrel on the other. Diesel models were virtually the same, especially in the case of the 300D, which only had a glowplug indicator above the barrel within the bank of warning lights and an idle screw control to the left of the column as differences. On four-cylinder diesels, the key was only used to run the glowplugs and accessories, with the engine start/stop function carried out by a push/pull knob to the left of the steering column that could also be twisted for idle control. The positioning of the latter was perhaps the only real ergonomic failing concerning the interior, and slowly but surely, the key-based start/stop feature on the 3-litre car was phased in on the other diesel models, leaving only the idle control and glowplug light as obvious differences.

Column controls consisted of a large stalk on the left (or right on rhd cars) that looked after indicators, headlight dip/main/flash control, wash/wipe activation and windscreen wiper speeds, and occasionally a cruise control wand on automatic cars fitted with this optional extra. On the opposite side to the four-spoke steering wheel, with a padded centre boss that sounded the horn when pushed on the outer edges, was a large glovebox with its own lock.

spawned by necessity back then were duly carried over and refined still further. It was necessary to look to the future and pay little heed to the past in this area of the W123's development.

As had become the norm at Mercedes during this period, the dashboard was basically a 'T' shape, with the lower part extending into a centre console that housed the gear selector before continuing back between the front seats. The decision to use a foot-operated parking brake allowed the rearmost oddments tray to become a truly useful item, and avoided a positioning clash on cars fitted with a centre armrest up front.

The final dashboard layout included three round gauges in the main instrument binnacle, with a combination meter to the left (monitoring fuel level, coolant temperature and oil pressure), a speedometer in the middle (with integral odometers), and a clock over to the right. Turn signal indicators sat either side of the speedo, while the bank of warning lights sat along the bottom of the binnacle with the dash lighting rheostat/trip reset button

Close-up of the light switch and handbrake release knob fitted to lhd cars. Note the tasteful wood trim piece, signalling this to be either a 280 or 280E model.

Centre console of one of the base cars, complete with automatic transmission, a Becker 'Europa' radio and air conditioning.

Below this was another plastic moulding that dressed underneath the dashboard and behind the upper section of the centre console. This flexible knee bolster was coloured to suit the interior, matching the door panels, and played host to the bonnet release. Interestingly, the inside bonnet release only partially did the job, as it made a second safety catch pop out from a gap in the radiator grille, and this had to be pulled before the bonnet could be raised.

There was a bank of switches (or blanking plates on basic cars) at the top of the centre console, which looked after things like interior lighting in the rear compartment, the heated rear screen, power sunroof (when fitted), et cetera, and below these were the main controls for the vastly improved heating and ventilation (HVAC) system. A slider controlled airflow direction, while rotary switches looked after the temperature for each side of the cockpit and booster fan speed – simple yet effective and efficient, the arrangement was a reflection of the care and attention to detail that had gone into all of the switchgear. Continuing down, we come to the radio slot, and then the ashtray with a lighter hidden inside.

As the tail of the 'T' extended over the transmission tunnel, the gear selector was nearest the engine (at least on the vast majority of cars – as it happens, there was also a column change available, but almost all W123 models came with a floor-mounted gearshift), and the hazard warning light switch aft of this. Cars with power windows had their lifts surrounding the big red hazard switch, and the optional heated seat switches and speaker fade control were also located in this area. Beyond this was a large storage tray, and like the upper part of the main dashboard, the centre console was finished in black, giving it a more integrated look.

The front seats were in the typical Mercedes mould, being huge armchairs, but somehow offering a lot more support than seemed possible looking at them; a height adjustment feature was available – standard on some cars, optional on others. Inertia reel seatbelts were integrated into the design, with the uppermost section winding back into the B-post to give a neat appearance. The other anchor was built into the seat frame, meaning that the belt positioning was unaffected by seat adjustment; while the adjustable head restraints were another safety feature. Standard trim was cloth, with MB-Tex vinyl, leather or velour offered as

A base saloon with regular cloth trim on the seats, a manual gearbox, and manual window winders. The 280s – and the coupés that followed – actually used a subtly different cloth (albeit with the same colour code) which featured small chevrons.

Velour upholstery on the rear seats. Note the different door trim that came with the velour option, the deep central armrest, manual window winder, and ashtray.

The rear bench seat trimmed in regular cloth, but on a car equipped with rear seatbelts and power windows. Note also the perforated roof lining and grab handle, the latter complete with a coat-hook on the rear pair.

options. The padded door furniture was kept simple to avoid protrusions into the cockpit, with flush, chrome-plated door release levers, armrests that acted as door pulls (extended on the passenger side, where it wouldn't interfere with the steering action), window winders on cars with manual lifts, and map pockets. The driver also had an internal remote adjustment facility for the driver's-side mirror, while the rearview mirror was some 25 per cent wider than before to enhance the view out the back.

In the rear, the bench seat came with a substantial folding armrest in the centre, and there was similar door furniture to that seen on the front passenger-side, except the map pocket was replaced by a large ashtray. A nice touch was the lidded first aid compartment located on the rear parcel shelf.

Continuing the inside story, we may as well take a look at the boot. As well as carrying the spare wheel, jack, toolkit and

warning triangle, it provided a massive amount of luggage space – around half a cubic metre (17.6 cubic foot) of it, in fact. Flat black paint was used on most surfaces, although the floor was trimmed, and fitted luggage could be specified to make the most of the space available.

Chassis overview

To allow a suitably extensive testing programme, a total of 50 prototypes were built during the early part of 1974. Naturally, these were used to test all manner of components, including body structure, but it was the chassis engineers, ably guided by Hans Scherenberg (the company's technical overlord until the

The huge trunk, seen here on a pre-production car with the optional fitted luggage set. It should be noted, however, that despite what catalogue photography might infer, the boot was lined with a rubber mat rather than carpet on the early cars.

A test hack, this one with East European looks, although others featured Rover-style headlights and a rather more traditional grille design – those with even the slightest knowledge of the industry would have figured out the manufacturer with ease.

end of 1977, when he retired, handing the reins over to Werner Breitschwerdt), who made the greatest use of the engineering mules.

The design brief passed down to engineers called for enhanced refinement and safety via the latest technology (not so difficult given Stuttgart's huge R&D budget), but also stipulated that they keep in mind a reduction in servicing time and repair costs through added simplicity wherever possible. With hindsight, the brief was a real sign of progress and modern thinking.

The suspension on the 'Fintail' models was basically a mild update of that used on the 'Ponton' range, although there were a number of major revisions introduced in time for the '/8' launch that then found their way in one form or another on to other Stuttgart thoroughbreds. Given the Daimler-Benz policy of gentle evolution rather than revolution, it's therefore not surprising to find that many of the W123's

Hans Scherenberg (left) retired as Chief Engineer in December 1977, handing the reins to Professor Werner Breitschwerdt, seen here on the right. Legendary head of the experimental department, Rudy Uhlenhaut had already retired in 1972, by the way.

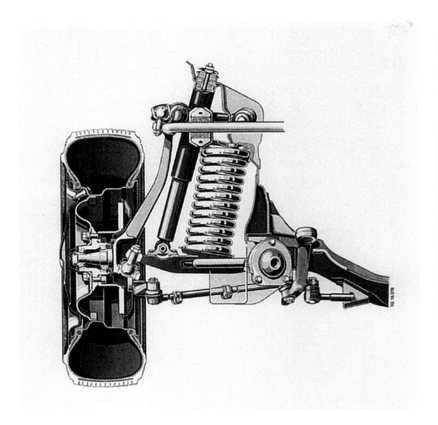

Front suspension.

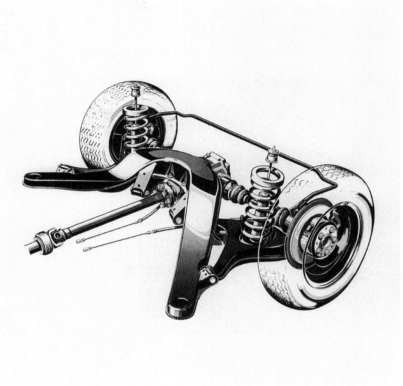

Rear suspension.

chassis components and their layout were already familiar to followers of Mercedes lore.

The front-end gained the new suspension from the contemporary S-Class, combining anti-dive and zero-offset (aka centre-point) steering geometry – the latter giving the car added stability under heavy braking, in the event of a blowout or during bad weather. Moving away from the traditional double-wishbone set-up, and also bolted directly to the bodyshell rather than a subframe on the W123, with refinement in all the connections assured by the use of rubber bushes, the system consisted of an upper control arm, located fore and aft by the anti-roll bar, which was bolted to the body at one end and the long steering knuckle at the other via a maintenance-free ball-joint. The double-acting gas-filled telescopic damper ran in a similar plane to the steering knuckle, bolting to the suspension turret in the engine bay at the top-end, and the lower control arm at the bottom. This control arm (effectively a built-up double-wishbone, thanks to

a support arm attached to the body) also provided a base for the coil spring, which was separated from the shock absorber and leaned forward and inward a touch. It was unusual, especially having the hefty anti-roll bar placed up high and following the line of the front bulkhead, but it was also effective, providing good handling and good NVH qualities.

Officially termed a 'diagonal pivot swing axle' within Mercedes circles, the independent rear suspension (IRS) was much the same as that of the W114/W115 and W116 models, and even the contemporary SL/SLC range. Huge, wide-based semi-trailing arms were attached at both sides to a substantial, boomerang-shaped suspension carrier, and then formed a seat for the coil spring and tube damper placed within it before attaching to the wheel carrier. The driveshafts ran aft of the main suspension, in a straight line with the rear axle, although the anti-roll bar was ultimately the rearmost component. The whole thing was then bolted to the body via the carrier,

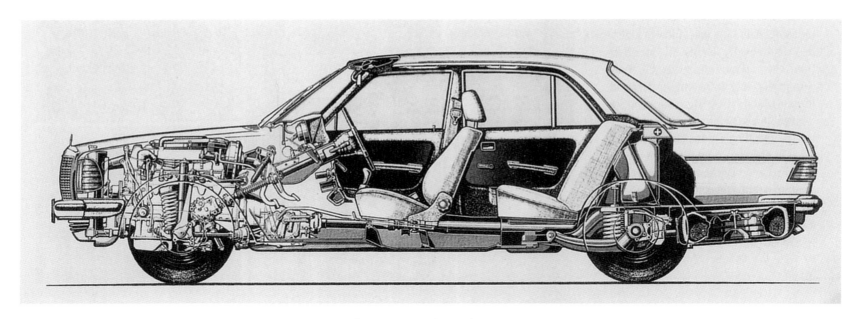

The W123's tight packaging.

the top of the shock absorbers, and the fixing points on the rubber-insulated anti-roll bar. Subtle revisions improved the car's handling, which, in conjunction with the wider track dimensions, enhanced stability and therefore active safety. A self-levelling rear suspension was available as an option, with special hydraulic globes fitted ahead of the axle line to look after ride height.

Not surprisingly, the tried-and-tested recirculating-ball steering system was called up for action yet again, having been a feature on Daimler-Benz road cars for longer than anyone cared to remember. The linkage had a hydraulic damper in the centre, and power-assistance (PAS) was available as an option on most cars, coming standard on the 280, 280E and 300D models. It should be mentioned here that the steering column was designed to buckle and move to the side in the event of a heavy accident, thus reducing the likelihood of it entering the cockpit following a frontal collision.

To save on production complications, and therefore reduce costs long-term, the braking system was the same for all cars, with vacuum servo-assisted discs all-round, a front/rear split circuit for added safety, and a stepped master cylinder arrangement.

The front discs were 278mm (10.9in) in diameter, while those at the rear were 279mm (11.0in) across, and incorporated

an integral drum with its own shoes to give a strong handbrake. Actually, handbrake isn't quite the right name, as it was a foot-operated parking brake on lhd cars, with the pedal tucked up in the far left-hand corner of the footwell in line with the regular pedal set (the latter featuring relocated hanger springs for added safety). The parking brake release was a small knob on left-hookers, linked to a chain rather than a rod, which eliminated the risk of metal piercing the cockpit during a heavy accident; right-hand drive machines had a larger pistol-grip handle, by the way, which brought the parking brake into action when pulled and had to be twisted to be released, but in either case, the arrangement did a superb job of cleaning up the appearance of the area around the transmission tunnel. Anyway, all four discs were teamed up with two-pot calipers that had a single piston on either side of the disc, and brake pad area was increased by a third; there was also a brake pad wear indictor added to the bank of dash warning lights.

As for the wheels and tyres, the 200, 230, 250 and the four diesel models had 175 SR14 tyres mounted on a 5.5J steel rim, while the 2.8-litre machines sported low-profile 195/70 HR14 rubber on a wider 6J rim. Alloy wheels would soon become available for those wishing to lighten the car's unsprung weight, or simply enhance its appearance.

A beautifully executed cutaway car based on the 280E, showing the vehicle's suspension, drivetrain and packaging from a rather different perspective.

The engine & gearbox line-up

Whilst looking outwardly similar to the powerplants dating back to the 'Ponton' model's glory days, a number of new engines had been introduced on the 'Stroke Eight' series in time for the 1974 season, so naturally the power-units used in the last of the W114/W115 cars and the contemporary S-Class provided the starting point for the W123's engine line-up, although each had a different code number according to its application. Interestingly, the production methods were changed on the W123, so that instead of lowering the body onto the drivetrain, as had been the norm on the older mid-size saloons, the longitudinally-mounted engine and transmission was lowered into the engine

bay, explaining why the bonnet was given its unusual 90 degree opening facility on the new cars.

Initially, at the time of the W123's announcement, two four-cylinder M115 petrol engines were listed, along with an all-new M123 six, two M110 six-cylinder petrol engines (one featuring CIS fuel-injection), a pair of OM615 diesel fours, an OM616 version of the four-cylinder diesel unit, and an unusual five-cylinder OM617 diesel powerplant. Going through them one at a time is probably easiest, as there are so many of them to cover.

Starting with the 115.938 unit used in the 200 models, this was a water-cooled straight-four with five main bearings in a grey cast iron block, and a single-overhead camshaft operating a single vertical inlet and exhaust valve via spring-loaded rocker arms for each pot in the aluminium alloy head. The 87.0mm x 83.6mm bore and stroke gave a displacement of 1988cc, and with a single Stromberg 175CDT carburettor and a 9.0:1 compression ratio, the petrol unit developed 94bhp at 4800rpm, along with 117lbft of torque at 3000rpm.

This was very similar to the powerplant used in the 200/8 (the 115.923), with a hydraulically-tensioned duplex chain running from the forged crankshaft all the way to the top of the engine to operate the camshaft, but also driving a small shaft with a bevel gear to drive the distributor and oil pump (the latter situated in the wet sump at the bottom of the engine); the water pump and cooling fan were looked after by a traditional vee-belt that took its power from the crankshaft pulley and also drove the alternator, which was sited close to the manifolds. Looking from the front of the engine, the distributor (fitted with regular points and a condensor) and casing for the cartridge-type oil filter were on the right, with the intake manifold opposite, and the exhaust manifold and starter motor below that. After a very simple two-into-one L-piece, the single pipe ran into a central muffler and a round-section backbox (featuring a stainless steel inner skin to prolong life), with a single exhaust pipe exiting from the nearside of the vehicle.

The 115.954 used in the 230 models was much the same as that found in the W123 200s, and likewise the 115.951 from the 230.4 '/8' model, although, again, it was 1bhp down on 'Stroke Eight' era output due to tuning that gave fractionally better fuel economy figures. The main difference

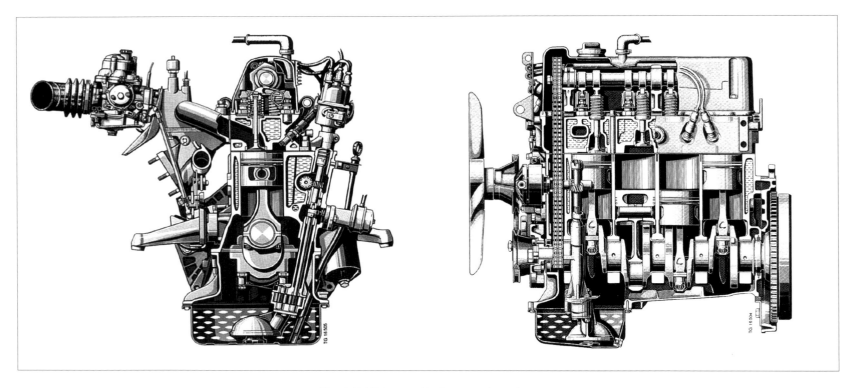

The M115 four-cylinder petrol engine.

compared to the 200 unit was an increase in the bore (taken out to measure 93.8mm), which in turn increased the cubic capacity to 2307cc. With everything else basically the same, the power-unit delivered a lazy 109bhp at 4800rpm, plus 137lbft of torque at 3000rpm.

The 2.5-litre M123 straight-six used in the 250 was next in line – the only truly new power-unit to grace the W123 range, as it took the place of the old 2.3-litre 120bhp M180 lump from the 230.6 and the 2.8-litre M130 from the previous 160bhp 250 model. As such, the car's designation on the tail of the new 250 was spot-on, as it was when the old M114 engine was still around!

The M123 unit was actually very similar to the M115 series in its basic construction and layout. Naturally, it had two extra cylinders and all that entailed, including a larger sump, and a viscous-coupled cooling fan, although there was some cost-cutting in the four-bearing bottom-end and the use of a single-row timing chain. With an 86.0mm bore and 72.5mm stroke (giving 2525cc), a single twin-choke Solex carburettor and

an 8.7:1 c/r, the engine gave 129bhp at 5500rpm, along with 145lbft of torque 2000rpm lower down the rev-range. For the record, the exhaust system consisted of twin pipes going into a centre box, from which a single pipe went into the backbox, and the tailpipe appearance was then the same as that of the 200 and 230 models.

Finally, as far as the petrol engines were concerned at least, there were the two 2.8-litre M110 units, which were basically lightly modified versions of the 160bhp 110.921 and 185bhp 110.981 engines from the '/8' series. The seven-bearing cast iron block was much like that of the M115 series, albeit with a wider sump like that found on the M123 unit, and the dipstick situated on the opposite side. In addition, the flat-top pistons found in the smaller-displacement engines were replaced by thoroughly modern items with a crown shaped to induce swirl in the air-fuel charge to encourage cleaner burning.

Above the pistons was an aluminium alloy crossflow head with a dohc arrangement, which was completely different to that of the lesser petrol engines, resembling the contemporary

The M123 six-cylinder petrol engine with a 4AT gearbox.

Jaguar XK twin-cam six in principle; the big difference between the Coventry engine and its Stuttgart counterpart was that the induction side was on the right looking from the front of engine on the M110, with the exhaust side on the left (this being the opposite of the XK layout). Anyway, the camshafts were driven by a duplex chain, and a single inlet and exhaust valve (with rocker arms adjusted by hydraulic tappets between the cams and

valve stems) were employed for each pot again, but now angled over so that they formed a vee shape in section, with a central sparkplug in the roof of the hemispherical combustion chamber – again, a la Jaguar practice.

As far as the Mercedes was concerned, the fuel delivery system was completely different, both to the 'Big Cat' and internally within the 280 range, with a twin-choke Solex being used for

The M110 six-cylinder petrol engine in carburettor guise.

The M110 six-cylinder petrol engine with fuel-injection. One can tell it's an early injected engine, because the air filter housing sits transversely on the fuel delivery system. The electric fan up front indicates this car has air conditioning.

the strict 280 (engine code 110.923) and Bosch K-Jetronic fuel-injection for the 280E – the latter using the 110.984 code, and the 'E' standing for 'Einspritzung', which is the German for injection. The 280E's mechanical indirect injection set-up, which improved emissions and economy, was complemented by electronic ignition and a viscous fan (as per the 280) – items that also helped in the fuel consumption stakes. Dual exhaust pipes were used on the 2.8-litre cars, incidentally, all the way from the manifold, through the centre and backbox, and ending in twin tailpipes.

In the background, while some countries called for reduced compression ratios to cope with their poor fuel quality, emissions were becoming increasingly strict in developed countries outside Europe. A catalytic converter was fitted to US- and Japan-bound vehicles, which seriously dented engine performance. For instance, the output on the detoxed 280E unit dropped to 142bhp, and was further reduced, to just 137bhp, on California- and Japan-specification cars, as the latter came with a pair of additional reduction cats. However, rather than look at these

now, we will tackle the export market machines in the chapters that follow.

And so we come to the water-cooled diesel engines. Again, they were based on the '/8' power-units, with the 200D and 220D employing OM615 fours (the 2-litre 615.940 was the replacement for the 55bhp 615.913 used in the 200D/8, while the 615.941 superceded the 615.912 found in the old 60bhp 220D/8 model), the 240D an OM616 (the four-cylinder 616.912 being the updated version of the 65bhp 616.916 unit used in the 'Stroke Eight' series), and the 300D an unusual OM617 five-cylinder powerplant – the 617.912 in the case of the W123 range.

The five-cylinder diesel engine was nothing new per se, but it was certainly new to the passenger car world. Having made its debut in 85bhp 617.910 guise in the W115 '/8' in

The OM615 four-cylinder diesel engine.

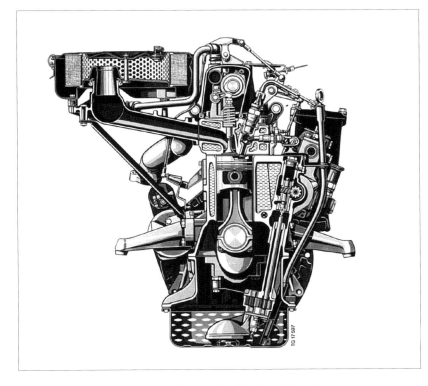

The OM616 four-cylinder diesel engine.

1974, with the car badged as a 240D 3.0 or 300D depending on the market, the timing couldn't have been better in view of the fuel crisis sparked off by the Arab-Israeli War (aka the Yom Kippur War) at the end of 1973, when the price of oil shot through the roof and fuel shortages at the pumps were commonplace. Ironically, it put Mercedes in a good position, as the crisis signalled the first rise of diesel power outside mainland Europe, and the unusual combination of frugality, power and refinement of the 3-litre five attracted a whole new clientele that would never have previously considered the idea of running a diesel car – the image of which was typically noisy and slow.

The basic construction and layout of the OM615 and OM616 was not dissimilar to the petrol fours, although both the head and block were made in cast iron, and the sparkplug position was taken by an injector nozzle. A duplex chain-driven single-overhead camshaft looked after the pair of vertical valves in each cylinder, and even the distributor drive was retained, albeit without the distributor, as it was used for the oil pump located in the narrow sump, alongside the dipstick. The four-plunger injection pump was on the right if one looked at the engine from the front, to the side of the high-mounted oil filter, while air was fed in from the left-hand side, above the exhaust manifold. Where the OM615 and OM616 differed the most was in the intake area, with the 2.4-litre engine having a far straighter air tract and a pancake air filter rather than a separate one sat in the corner of the engine bay, almost alongside the radiator shroud; the 240D lump also gained the more-responsive mechanical fuel governing system and key 'ignition' already found on the flagship, 3-litre diesel model. Going back to basics, the fixed cooling fan was driven by a vee-belt off the crankshaft – which, incidentally, ran in five main bearings.

These three variants were closely related in bore/stroke relationships, too. The 200D unit had a 87mm bore and 83.6mm stroke to give a 1988cc displacement; the 220D shared the same bore but a longer 92.4mm stroke to obtain a 2197cc cubic capacity, while the 240D came with the same stroke as the 220D but a larger 91.0mm bore to give a 2404cc displacement. Each had a 21.0:1 compression ratio, with the 200D developing 55bhp and 83lbft of torque, the 220D

Continued page 61

57

The OM617 five-cylinder
diesel engine.

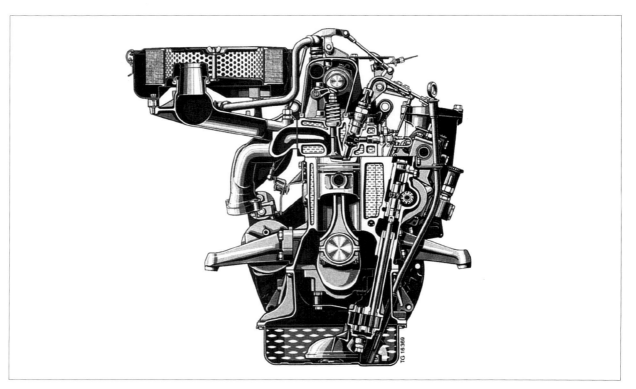

Above and overleaf: A final bit of torture testing at the works, but it was too late to change anything now – commitment to the W123 project was made …

The finished product. A pre-production model that was maintained in pristine condition to allow it to be used for catalogue photography and members of the press.

60bhp and 93lbft, and the 240D 65bhp and 101lbft – in all cases, maximum power was delivered at 4200rpm, and peak torque at 2400rpm.

The OM617 was basically the same as the OM616 with an extra cylinder tacked on to the end. Other than the obvious changes needed to allow for the fifth cylinder, about the only significant difference compared to the OM616 was the head design on the intake side, a heavier flywheel, and a viscous-coupled cooling fan; even the oil sump was similar in size.

With a 91.0mm bore and 92.4mm stroke (shared with the 240D), giving a capacity of 3005cc, and a 21.0:1 c/r, the 3-litre unit developed 80bhp at 4200rpm, along with 127lbft of torque at 2400rpm. All the diesel cars had the same basic exhaust system, with a single downpipe running into a central silencer, then a round-section back-box before exiting on the nearside of the vehicle.

As for the transmissions, all cars were available with a choice of four-speed manual (4MT) or four-speed automatic epicyclic

auto
motor
und
sport
Heft 22 25.Oktober 1975 DM 2.50 E 1418 DX
NEU
Der
kleine Mercedes
DA-DU 167
Porsche Jahrgang 1976
Test 911 und Carrera
Airbag-Versuche
Besser als der Gurt?
Porsche-Interview
Kommt das Langzeitauto?
Konkurrenz für den Rekord?
Test Opel Ascona
Konkurrenz für Mercedes?
Test Peugeot 604
extra
Autofahrer-Programme 1975/76
Reisen in den Winter

Some people just couldn't wait. This is the cover of *Auto Motor und Sport* from October 1975.

(4AT) gearboxes, the latter being an optional extra, of course, and coming with a torque converter rather than the older fluid coupling.

It's fair to say that both came with a central floor-mounted selector (the manual shift having reverse up and to the left, with first through fourth in an 'H' pattern to the right of it, while the automatic came with the staggered gate that hardly anyone has been able to improve on to this day), although it should be noted that there was actually a manual column-change available for official taxi conversions shipped to Finland and a handful of police cars, and also a column-change selector for automatic gearboxes, but the latter is very rare indeed, as it wasn't available in the majority of export markets, including the US and Japan. Power was taken from the back of the gearbox via a three-piece propshaft, which then connected to the rear axle, with hypoid bevel gears transferring power to the driveshafts attached to the rear wheels.

With so many engines, naturally the gearbox variations were huge. Starting with the manual transmission, the 200, 230 and 250 and all four diesel models used the G76/18C unit (code 716.005), with 3.90 on first, 2.30 on second, 1.41 on third, and a direct top. The 200, 200D and 220D employed a 3.92:1 rear axle ratio, the 230, 250 and 240D a 3.69:1 version, and the 300D a taller 3.46:1 ratio. Meanwhile, the 280 and 280E made use of the G76/18B gearbox (716.001), which had the same internal ratios as the 18C unit, but was combined with a 3.54:1 back axle. Incidentally, the clutch was a traditional single dry-plate unit.

Things were more complicated on the automatic front, although the W4B025 type number was consistent, as were the 3.98, 2.39, 1.46 and 1.00 internal ratios across the range. However, due to the brake bands and other fine-tuning, virtually every model had its own code number applied. The 200 employed the 722.115 unit, the 230, the 722.119, the 250, the 722.113, the strict 280, the 722.111, the 280E, the 722.112, the 200D and 220D, the 722.116, the 240D, the 722.117, and the 300D, the 722.118; final-drive ratios were the same as those specified on the manual cars. It's perhaps worth noting here that *Autocar*, amongst several other respected journals, rated the Daimler-Benz automatic gearbox as "the best currently available" when the W123 was being launched. Incidentally, standing starts were usually accomplished on second gear, aiding economy, unless one activated the kickdown mode with a heavy right foot.

No turning back

The extensive road testing programme got under way during September 1974, following on from a round of successful crash tests that involved over 3000 hours of work, and while the new car was basically ready for production by the following spring (winter testing had been completed in Sweden during February), there was no hurry to get the W123 to the marketplace, simply because the '/8' models were still selling exceptionally well. The continued popularity of the 'Stroke Eight' range allowed the Daimler-Benz engineers more time to perfect the W123 on all fronts before series production started in a limited way during November 1975, when the first 280 and 280E models were put together. However, no prices were released until 27 January 1976, when Helmut Schmidt (then head of sales) announced the full range at the international press launch held at Bandol (to the east of Marseille) in southern France. The next chapter looks at the first production models, taking in all of the major markets along the way …

4
Early production models

After years of running countless model variations alongside each other – some, like the W111 two-door models, lasting six years beyond their four-door counterparts – the introduction of the W123 series saloons in January 1976 brought with them a sense of calm. Although a few of their '/8' predecessors were allowed to continue for a little while longer, compared with other model changeovers it was a clean progression this time around. From now on, the W123s would take up the mid-range slot (as what would become known as the E-Class in future generations), the saloons, duly followed by coupé and estate models, augmenting the S-Class saloons at the top of the line, and the SL/SLC sports cars.

The first batch of W123 models included no fewer than nine saloons for the domestic market. As noted in the previous chapter, this was an era when the model designations on the bootlid tended to make sense, so a 200 was a 2-litre saloon with a petrol engine, while the 'D' suffix implied a diesel powerplant was lurking under the bonnet – a 3-litre lump in the case of the 300D, for instance. The only oddity was the 280E, with the 'E' appendage denoting the use of a fuel-injected petrol engine.

When the January 1976 price list was released, it showed that the 200 was introduced at DM 18,382 in manual guise, with the 200D a touch more at DM 18,870. The 230 was next up, commanding DM 19,203, with the 220D DM 355 more, while the 240D was announced at DM 20,146. The 250, with its straight-six, was priced at DM 21,767, and the flagship diesel – the 300D – at DM 22,311. The 2.8-litre cars were significantly more expensive, with the 280 saloon pegged at DM 24,997, and the fuel-injected 280E at DM 26,895 – a premium of almost 50 per cent on the base 200 model.

Standard equipment included disc brakes all-round, gas-filled shock absorbers, front and rear anti-roll bars, a safety steering column, steering damper, long-life exhaust system, underseal and

Continued page 67

Nearly 2000 cars had been made by the time of the launch, mostly 280s and 280Es, allowing dealers to have demonstrator vehicles on hand as soon as the W123 made its debut.

Above and top left: The 200 saloon, which tipped the scales at 1340kg (2948lb) according to DIN measurements. In reality, of course, a car on the driveway, ready to roll, was far heavier – typically around 200kg (440lb) more. Top right: tail of the 200D saloon.

Front and rear three-quarter views of an early 230 saloon.

220 D Durch das größere Hubvolumen von 2197 cm³ leistet dieser 4-Zylinder-Diesel 60 PS/DIN (44 kW). Die Spitzengeschwindigkeit von 135 km/h ist gleichzeitig auch Dauergeschwindigkeit. Damit erreicht der 220 D auf langen Strecken hohe Durchschnitts-Reisegeschwindigkeiten. Ein bewährtes, robustes Aggregat. Die Vorkammer-Einspritzung gibt ihm die gute Elastizität und erstaunliche Laufruhe. Das Fahrwerk ist so ausgelegt, daß es weit höheren Motorleistungen - beispielsweise denen des 280 E mit 177 PS/DIN - gerecht wird.

Catalogue page for the 220D, and the badging on the tail. Officially, this model weighed 1380kg (3036lb).

wax pumped into cavities to conserve the body, a diagnostics connector for petrol-engined cars, integrated front foglights, automatic headlight adjustment to allow for load, parking lights (with a left/right switch), a rear foglight, twin reversing lights, a wash/wipe system with three-speed wipers, laminated safety glass on the front and side screens, a heated rear screen, full carpeting, cloth trim, three-point automatic seatbelts and adjustable headrests on the front seats, a quartz clock, oil pressure gauge, driver's-side mirror with interior adjustment, breakaway rearview mirror, sunvisors, separate heating controls, a lockable glovebox with courtesy light, a centre console with ashtray/cigarette lighter in front of the gearlever and an oddments tray aft of it, a folding rear centre armrest, armrests on all four doors (extended on passenger doors), map pockets on the front doors and ashtrays on the rear ones, childproof locks, overhead handgrips above passenger doors, a warning triangle, and first aid box.

Above and top left: The 240D saloon, loaded with optional extras like the headlight wash/wipe system and rear headrests.

Above and top right: The 1976 250 saloon.

The 280 and 280E saloons came with halogen headlights and front foglights, different bumper trim, power-assisted steering, Zebrano wood-style garnishing pieces on the dashboard, seat height adjustment for the driver, and cloth inserts on the inner door panels, while the diesels came with stronger battery specifications – a 55Ah unit was the norm on petrol-engined cars (albeit 44Ah on the 200 base model), but the 200D had a 66Ah one, and the larger diesel engines commanded an 88Ah

battery. For the record, the 300D also featured power-assisted steering.

The first catalogue featuring the 2.8-litre machines noted alloy wheels (SA code 640, priced at DM 1554), automatic transmission (SA 420, at DM 1610), self-levelling suspension (SA 480, at DM 744), air-conditioning (SA 580, at DM 2664), a manually- (SA 411) or power-operated (SA 410) sunroof (priced at DM 766 and DM 1021, respectively), central locking (SA 466, at DM 311), power windows (SA 583 for the front windows

Left and below: A 300D that was used in one of the first W123 road tests, and a detail shot of the badge on the tail of the 3-litre diesel models.

only, at DM 577, or SA 584 for all four, priced at DM 1043), seat heaters (SA 873/872, at DM 422 for the front or rear pair), orthopaedic seats (SA 404/405 or SA 406 for both seats, at DM 83 per side), and a fire extinguisher (SA 682 at DM 53) as options, along with the usual choice of stereo equipment, and paint and trim upgrades.

On the subject of stereo equipment, Becker radios were the norm during this period. Early offerings included the 'Grand Prix' stereo radio (SA code 516, priced at DM 821), the 'Mexico' radio/cassette unit (SA 511, at DM 1576), the 'Monza' cassette player (SA 510, at DM 844, or SA 258 at DM 910 if a traffic news feature was included), and the 'Europa' radio (SA 514, at DM 555, or SA 257 at DM 622 with traffic news). On top of this, one had to allow for the rear parcel shelf-mounted speakers (SA 812, at DM 244), while aerials included an automatic one supplied with a radio (SA 531, at DM 327), the same thing without a radio (SA 532, at DM 405), a manual aerial without a radio (SA 534, at DM 78), and for those who preferred their own stereo, there was also a chance to have the audio preparation done without a radio (SA 533) for DM 94.

Special paint added DM 222 to the invoice, incidentally, while metallic shades cost the buyer a hefty DM 982. Other options at this time included power steering for base cars (SA code 422, at DM 644), cruise control for AT cars (SA 440,

Above and top: A 280 saloon on the road, and a detail shot of the rear of the same car. The 280 weighed in at 1455kg (3201lb), 15kg (33lb) less than the fuel-injected model.

at DM 389), tinted glass (SA 591, at DM 250, or SA 590 with a laminated windscreen, at DM 455), a passenger-side door mirror (SA 502, at DM 94), all-weather tyres (SA 645, at DM 144), halogen headlights for the base cars (SA 618, at DM 72, but quickly made standard across the board on EU-spec cars at the start of 1977), a headlight wash/wipe system (SA 600, at DM 416), a heated rear screen with laminated safety glass (SA 248, at DM 128), two-tone horn (SA 452, at DM 178), MB-Tex vinyl trim at a DM 178 premium, velour trim at DM 1404, leather trim at DM 1598, seat height adjustment (SA 571/572, at DM 83 per side), reinforced front seats (SA 561/562, at DM 26 per side), a pair of rear headrests (SA 430, at DM 150), rear compartment lighting with door contacts (SA 876, at DM 61), a set of three rear seatbelts (SA 435, at DM 189), a folding armrest between the front seats (SA 570, at DM 144), luggage nets on the back of the front seats (SA 286, at DM 50), a glovebox lock (SA 542, at DM 21), coconut floormats (SA 835, at DM 139), a seven-piece luggage set (SA 285, although later listed as an accessory rather than an

Above and overleaf: An early 280E dealing with the snow, and a second car fitted with alloy wheels. For a little while, the Fuchs alloys would be as rare as hen's teeth, but supplies eventually began filtering through at the expected rate.

The options page from the first W123 catalogue.

ex-works option, at DM 988), an uprated battery (SA 673, at DM 42, although standard on the diesel-engined models), and a towbar (SA 550, at DM 461). There was even a Becker mobile phone installation, but with a DM 13,500 price-tag, it was unlikely to have attracted many buyers, and rubber mats (SA 837) could be chosen rather than the standard floormats for no extra cost.

Colour & trim summary

A great deal of confusion exists with regard to standard paint colour names, and especially trim and upholstery designations, where the same moniker was often used for a different shade. Depending on the year, ordering material by name only could result in the wrong hue being supplied, and some countries used different names altogether, so this list should help those looking to restore a car to original specification.

January 1976 – September 1979

Standard solid paint colours

No	German name	English name	Other names
040	Schwarz	Black	–
470	Coloradobeige	Colorado Beige	–
504	Englischrot	English Red	–
606	Ahorngelb	Maple Yellow	–
737	Classicweiss	Classic White	–
867	Kaledoniengrün	Caledonia Green	–
903	Blau	Blue	–
922	Pastellblau	Pastel Blue	–

Special solid paint colours

No	German name	English name	Other names
406	Cayenneorange	Cayenne Orange	–
424	Topasbraun	Topaz Brown	–
516	Mittelrot	Medium Red	–
568	Signalrot	Signal Red	–
618	Mimosengelb	Mimosa Yellow	–
623	Hellelfenbein	Light Ivory	–
624	Gelb	Yellow	–
673	Saharagelb	Sahara Yellow	–
740	Pastellgrau	Pastel Grey	–
825	Tiefgrün	Deep Green	–
870	Nickelgrün	Nickel Green	–
904	Dunkelblau	Dark Blue	Midnight Blue

Metallic paint colours

No	German name	English name	Other names
172	Anthrazitgrau	Anthracite Grey	–
404	Milanbraun	Milan Brown	–
419	Ikonengold	Icon Gold	–

No	German name	English name	Other names
525	Brilliantrot	Brilliant Red	–
735	Astralsilber	Astral Silver	–
861	Silbergrün	Silver-Green	–
874	Citrusgrün	Citrus Green	–
876	Zypressengrün	Cypress Green	–
906	Graublau	Grey-Blue	–
931	Magnetitblau	Magnetite Blue	–

Cloth trim

No	German name	English name	Other names
001	Schwarz	Black	–
002	Blau	Blue	–
003	Tabak	Tobacco	–
004	Bambus	Bamboo	–
005	Pergament	Parchment	Mushroom
006	Moos	Moss Green	–

Vinyl trim

No	German name	English name	Other names
101	Schwarz	Black	–
102	Blau	Blue	–
103	Tabak	Tobacco	–
104	Bambus	Bamboo	–
105	Pergament	Parchment	Mushroom
106	Moos	Moss Green	–

Leather trim

No	German name	English name	Other names
201	Schwarz	Black	–
202	Blau	Blue	–
203	Tabak	Tobacco	–

No	German name	English name	Other names
204	Bambus	Bamboo	–
205	Pergament	Parchment	Mushroom
206	Moos	Moss Green	–

Velour trim			
No	**German name**	**English name**	**Other names**
901	Anthrazit	Anthracite	Black
902	Blau	Blue	–
903	Tabak	Tobacco	–
904	Bambus	Bamboo	–
905	Pergament	Parchment	Mushroom
906	Moos	Moss Green	–

An early saloon in use as a taxi. There are still a huge number of W123 taxis in service, especially in places like Africa and the Southern Mediterranean countries.

It wasn't until February 1976 that full-scale production of the 200, 230, 200D, 220D, 240D, 300D models started, with the 250 following in April. By this time, a number of minor changes had already been applied to the W123, with the glovebox lock receiving attention, and the steel road wheels gaining some additional holes to help disperse heat from the brakes that much better. In April, the model line received improved seatbelt buckles and the bonnet support was made stronger, while May saw the adoption of a new interior light, modified to reduce glare. As it happens, the seatbelts were looked at again at the end of summer, and once more at the beginning of autumn. Actually, it's worth noting here that wearing a front seatbelt became compulsory in Germany on the first day of 1976, although the fitting of front seatbelts to new cars had been law since 1970; rear seatbelts were not required until the rules changed in 1979, and even then, no-one was forced to wear them for several years.

During September 1976, the floorpan and crossmember design was modified to allow a catalytic converter installation to be fitted on US-bound cars – a definite sign of the times. In the same month, a second motor damper was added on 300D models to improve refinement, and a few days later the radiator fan fairing was modified via a change in the material selected. Not long after, in November 1976, the black rubber dressing piece behind the front bumper was extended upwards to sit higher on the sheetmetal below the headlight

units, while all cars inherited reinforced rear door hinges in December.

From the end of January 1977, the three-pointed star on the bootlid sat a fraction flatter than before, and H4 halogen headlights became standard on all W123 models. Domestic prices increased by an average of around four per cent in the following month, taking the 200 saloon up to DM 19,025, and the flagship 280E model up to DM 28,116.

Finally, in March 1977, a new fuel tank sender unit was adopted, allowing a larger reserve, and a cladding piece was added to divide the fuel tank and luggage space. In addition, the cover on the window cranks was changed to a hard plastic version, and the treadplate design was revised.

The W123 performed well in road tests, generating praise from all quarters.

The W123 was well-received by press and public alike. Writing at the time of the launch, *Motor Trend*'s Mike Knepper said: "The 280E and the six-cylinder engine really come into their own on the high-speed Autobahns. I joyfully covered long stretches of beautiful, smooth pavement with the speedometer hovering around the 200kph mark. At that speed there was a good bit of wind noise, but that's my only complaint. Directional stability was perfect, road feel was what it should be, and the car simply exuded its capabilities as a piece of engineering excellence."

Whilst not disputing the existence of London Taxi-style sounds and smells from outside the car, Knepper was impressed by the 300D, too, stating: "The five-cylinder engine is extremely smooth. In fact, it's so smooth, quiet and relatively strong, it's easy to forget you're driving a diesel at all. From inside, it might be a small American V8 working along, it's that good."

Even the 200 had its fans, with Britain's *Motor* magazine commenting: "A day's drive on German roads left no doubt that the latest 200 is not only more refined than its predecessor, but that the changes to instrumentation, ventilation and general styling have all been very worthwhile. The car is sluggish, but the excellent handling inspires great confidence."

Perhaps not surprisingly, according to a contemporary article in *Auto, Motor und Sport*, given that the waiting list on domestic deliveries had already stretched to over a year by the time the 1977 season arrived, demand for the new car was such that a black market had grown up around it. Reports of DM 5000 premiums being paid for new or even lightly used saloons were

Above and right: A W123 out on the open road. A huge waiting list meant this was nothing more than a dream for many eager buyers in 1976 and 1977...

commonplace in the press, proving the instant success of the W123 series beyond doubt.

The US market

The W123 cars finally arrived in the States in December 1976 as late 1977 MY machines. Due to the increasingly strict Federal emissions regulations, American buyers were restricted to a choice of just four saloons initially – the 230 (which delivered 86bhp SAE in US-spec, a drop of 7bhp on earlier '/8' models), the fuel-injected 280E (with 142bhp on tap), the 62bhp 240D, and the 77bhp 300D. Both petrol-engined models were fitted with catalytic converters, with the Californian version of the 280E gaining a couple of reduction cats in addition to the main unit. This set-up drained another 5bhp, but with the Golden State being such an important market, the demands of the local government – which ultimately eliminated the 230 from the west coast – could not be ignored. And in the end, anything aimed at

The legend continues...

Mercedes-Benz presents a singular new achievement.

Announcing an important new design from Mercedes-Benz. Sleek. Lean. With nimble handling. Ample space for five adults. Dozens of ingenious safety provisions. And fuel-injected power plants. The new Mercedes-Benz: Engineered like no other car in the world.

The new Mercedes-Benz required a full eight years to perfect. That may seem an almost leisurely pace.

However, when you come to understand the importance of this new Mercedes-Benz design, and the significance of its many engineering innovations, you'll see that it couldn't have been produced any faster.

New suspension

The design concept of the new Mercedes-Benz represents an exquisite balance among the needs for occupant protection, refined handling characteristics, and driver comfort. Maximizing each of these qualities required particular engineering finesse.

Perhaps the major achievement is the new front suspension. It is a simplified and strengthened front-end construction, buttressed with special gas-pressurized shock absorbers. It helps

Three distinctive models. Each one is fuel injected. One of them will meet your precise driving requirements.

240D	300D	280E
• Engine Type—Diesel, 4-cylinder, fuel injection, overhead camshaft, 5 main bearings	• Engine Type—Diesel, 5-cylinder, fuel injection, overhead camshaft, 6 main bearings	• Engine Type—6-cylinder, continuous fuel injection, double overhead camshafts, 7 main bearings
• Displacement—146.7 cu. in.	• Displacement—183.4 cu. in.	• Displacement—167.6 cu. in.
• Fuel/Fuel System—Diesel #2, mechanical fuel injection	• Fuel/Fuel System—Diesel #2, mechanical fuel injection	• Breakerless, transistorized ignition system
• Manual Transmission— 4-speed, fully synchronized	• Automatic Transmission— 4-speed, torque converter	• Automatic Transmission— 4-speed, torque converter
• Curb Weight—3210 lbs.	• Curb Weight—3515 lbs.	• Curb Weight—3530 lbs.
• Overall Height—56.6"	• Overall Height—56.6"	• Overall Height—56.6"
• Overall Length—190.9"	• Overall Length—190.9"	• Overall Length—190.9"
• Turning Circle—37'	• Turning Circle—37'	• Turning Circle—37'
• Trunk Capacity—17.7 cu. ft.	• Trunk Capacity—17.7 cu. ft.	• Trunk Capacity—17.7 cu. ft.
• Passengers—5	• Passengers—5	• Passengers—5
• Wheelbase—110"	• Wheelbase—110"	• Wheelbase—110"

the new Mercedes-Benz deliver precise steering with instant response, virtually no lean in braking or cornering—and straight-line control on even the roughest roads. What's more, the lubricated-for-life ball joints are completely maintenance free.

There are dual-circuit power disc brakes on all four wheels—just as there have been on all Mercedes-Benz automobiles since 1968.

The look of the future

This new design is a fresh look for Mercedes-Benz. Closer to the road.

Slightly wider. Clean-limbed. The new effect is subtle but undeniable.

Inside, there's new luxuriousness, with ample front and rear legroom and headroom. And the trunk offers 17.7 cubic feet of usable space.

A perceptive observer may notice that all the frame members supporting the roof seem more slender than in previous Mercedes-Benz models. Actually, these crucial safety members have been strongly reinforced. And their slim shape contributes to driver visibility. Another visibility aid: a total of 27.3 square feet of tinted glass.

The passenger compartment is a steel shell surrounded by lateral-impact-resistant elements, with crushable safety zones in front and rear.

The front safety zones are now creased for even more precisely defined deformation should an accident occur.

The rear crush path has been lengthened by moving the gas tank forward to a protected position above the rear axle.

And in front, the steering mechanism is positioned well behind the front wheels to protect it in a collision.

The aesthetics of safety

Study the dashboard's well-thought-through details and take pleasure in them. The sense of stark elegance. The intelligent arrangement of switches and controls. The impressively sized steering wheel with a built-in safety chest pad. Anatomically designed seats.

Impact-resistant handles on all doors.

Fore and aft, a new type of energy-absorbing bumper flows smoothly into the car's silhouette.

The new Mercedes-Benz is, quite possibly, a masterpiece. A cursory look will indicate that. But only when you take the wheel will you recognize the significant difference between this and all other cars. Arrange a drive with your authorized Mercedes-Benz Dealer. Then you'll agree: the legend continues.

Mercedes-Benz
Engineered like no other car in the world.
©Mercedes-Benz, 1976

American advertising from 1976.

keeping the air clean has to be applauded, even if sometimes the intent was stronger than the actual results – the rise of diesel power, accounting for almost half of US sales at the time, was in response to one thing at the cost of another, with a blind eye being turned to particulate matter (PM) from the exhaust and NOx emissions, while catalytic converters had almost as many minus points against them as plus points. Anyway, in another bow to market demands, only the 240D was available with a manual transmission, with the other

three cars coming with an automatic gearbox only (the 4AT unit was available as an option on the 240D).

Visual differences included larger, impact-absorbing bumpers (adding 125mm/4.9in to the car's overall length), and unique, sealed beam circular headlights based on the European entry-level model design; inside, the use of labels rather than symbols on the switchgear made for a novel contrast compared to the ROW cars. At the time of the launch, the saloons were priced at $11,346 (POE) for the manual 240D, $12,264 for the

77

A second piece of early US advertising, this one concentrating on the 280E saloon. Note the automatic air conditioning controls on the dashboard drawing.

230, $15,791 for the 300D, and $16,290 for the 280E. Prices started at $19,030 for the contemporary S-Class range, the entry-level model sharing the same engine as the flagship of the W123 line.

Being well-engineered and full of standard amenity features like PAS, central locking, tinted glass, driver's-seat height adjustment, plus air-conditioning, power windows, cruise control, an armrest between the front seats and a stereo radio on the 280E and 300D grades, most contemporary reports were very complimentary Stateside, with *Motor Trend* even declaring the 280E 'Import Car Of The Year', despite it being the highest-priced vehicle amongst the nominations – a fact that was hard to avoid given the increasing value of the Deutschmark. "Simple overall excellence provided the winning margin for the new Mercedes-Benz sedan," said the magazine.

After recording a 0-60 time of 12.3 seconds (18.9 seconds over the standing-quarter) and an observed top speed of 109mph (174kph), David E. Davis Jr of *Car & Driver* noted on the 280E: "The Mercedes almost seems to dramatize the fact that it is a machine – a pleasant, comfortable machine, but a machine nevertheless – not a boudoir, or some mobile extension of your living room. It is solid and fast, it feels as safe as a house, and I'd like to own one. I guess that's what it's all about." Most of his colleagues were full of praise for the car, too.

On the other hand, Patrick Bedard was not quite so impressed and brought some balance to reams and reams of gushing words: "This sedan is purposeful, solidly built, and incredibly direct in its responses. You do not spend days making its acquaintance. Five blocks, and you're ready to run with it; the tougher the conditions, the better. It is truly a pleasure on the cratered streets of New York where the confines are tight and the traffic unforgiving.

"But along with this directness you get a strong dose of militant machine. The 280E's engine is loud, the Michelin XVS treads sing against the pavement, wind noise takes over at speed and the automatic transmission shifts when it gets good and ready and not before. I'm fascinated by the intensity of this machine and knowing the willy-nilly tastes of most auto makers, I admire Daimler-Benz for having the courage of its convictions. Still, I do not share many of those convictions and, had I been responsible for the design of this car, it would not make such an assault upon the senses."

Country codes

All cars had a plate under the bonnet containing useful information, including original engine and transmission details and paintwork colour, as well as three-digit option codes. Not all options were listed, of course, otherwise it would have to be a huge plate on many vehicles, but within these codes, country identifiers were slipped in, along with Model Year numbers from 1980 onwards (800 stood for the 1980 season, 801 for 1981, and so on). Listed below are some of the more common country codes:

491	North American specification
492	California (US) specification
498	Japanese specification
620	Italian specification
622	UK specification
625	Australian specification
629	French specification

There were also a few other interesting codes, such as 820 for tourist deliveries (mainly US customers that picked their car up at the factory), 450 for a taxi, 970 for a police car, and so on. The main thing here, though, is to make people aware that not all the codes on the plate relate to options (combination codes are sometimes employed, too), and, in some cases, it's worth noting that a car has been built to satisfy regulations that may not suit its current location.

The UK market

Mercedes-Benz (UK) Limited may not have had a big stand at the 1976 Earls Court Motor Show at the end of October compared to the Ford one next to it, but the content was nonetheless important, for the London event marked the public debut of the W123 series in Britain.

While the old '/8' saloons ranged in price from £4475 for the 200 up to £6709 for the 280E, the W123 models were significantly more expensive. Prices started at £4940 including taxes on the 200, with the 200D at £5166, the 230 at £6375, the 240D at £6565, the 250 at £6965 (a fraction cheaper than the 'Stroke Eight' 280CE coupé), the 300D at £7600, and the flagship 280E at £7990. This meant that the 220D and strict 280 were left out of the UK line-up, although there were still an awful lot of '/8' variants listed at this time as well.

Following its test of an automatic 280E (the manual gearbox was a special order item on this model in the UK), *Autocar* declared the newcomer to be an "excellent performer provided one revs the very willing engine." It had "excellent brakes, steering, ride and handling," and was "comfortable and on the whole refined." Ultimately, despite the hefty £8000 price-tag, even before options like upgraded paint and trim, seatbelts (yes, still an option in the UK!), cruise control (£135), power windows (£199), a power sunroof (£349), air-conditioning (£899), a headlamp wash/wipe system (£136) and audio equipment were fitted, and competitors like the £6660 Jaguar XJ6 and £4750 3.5-litre SD1 Rover around, the magazine still felt that the car "was probably worth the money. All in all, the 280E is an impressive piece of motor vehicle engineering, modernized in all the best ways, yet clearly owing a lot to Mercedes traditions."

Interestingly, the same magazine warmed to the 300D, too. Recording a 0-60 time of 20.8 seconds and a top speed of 90mph (145kph), which is painfully slow by today's standards, the testers noted: "On paper, the performance may seem restricted, but in practice you find that faster cars are often overtaken. It is a comfortable, and, except when accelerating hard, a quiet car. £7600 is a lot of money to pay for any car these days – but then, there is nothing quite like driving a Mercedes-Benz."

An early right-hand drive car at speed.

As if things weren't complicated enough, it should be noted here that a lot of the early UK-spec cars broke the rule of thumb on the use of grille types covering the bulkhead vents. The author has seen many contemporary pictures, and it appears most of the early cars were sold with chrome dressing pieces, regardless of their engine, although the basic rules were duly followed as soon as the 1983 season changes came about.

Australia & Japan

As in the UK, the W123 series models were significantly more expensive than their '/8' predecessors Down Under. As an example, both the 230/6 and 240D were priced at around $15,500 in 1975, while prices started at almost $23,000 for the new saloon line-up. The W123 range was eventually released in Australia in November 1976, meaning they were classed – just about – as 1977 season models. The 230 was the base car, listed at $22,940 with automatic transmission, while the 250 was $24,740, and the diesel 300D $25,325. The automatic 280E was the flagship of the line, commanding $27,730 at a time when the 450SEL was $39,300 – about $1000 more than the shorter-wheelbase 450SE.

The W123 models landed in Japan around the same time, with the importers sticking to the same line-up as that found across the Pacific in the USA. They ranked alongside the 280S, 280SE, 450SE, 450SEL, 450SL and 450SLC in their first year, looking much like European-spec vehicles, but being powered by American-spec engines. DIN power outputs were quoted, so the 230 delivered 90bhp, the 280E 145bhp, the 240D 65bhp, and the 300D 80bhp.

Continued page 85

メルセデス・ベンツ

伝統の中に改めて開花した 新次元の車づくり

1972年のSLシリーズに次いで、翌年発表されたSクラス・シリーズには、新次元の車づくりを示唆するものとして、世界中の称賛が浴せられました。

中でも評価を受けたのは、その高度な安全性です。特に、"守り"の安全性だけに止めず、前向きのもの、つまりアクシデントを回避するための車の能力向上に正面から取り組み、これを確立したことが絶賛されました。これは、車をあくまで高速トランスポーテーションの手段として機能させるという前提での安全対策であり、メルセデス・ベンツは、鮮かにその回答を示したのです。

Sクラスに次いでデビューしたニュー・コンパクトサイズ・シリーズでも、その回答は同様に再現されています。つまり、メルセデス・ベンツ・シリーズは、実際にそれだけの速度が出る出ないに拘わらず、ハイクルージング・レベルで、天候や路面状況に影響されずに容易な操縦・快適な乗り心地が楽しめる"高速安全車"を目指して設計されているのです。このような安全リミットの高さは、日々のドライブで、常に全裕を感じさせます。これこそ、まさに「生きた安全性」といえるものではないでしょうか。

230 (C-123023)

280E (C-123033)

240D (123123)

NEW COMPACT SEDAN 230

穏健な性格。しかし十二分な機能を備えた、ベーシック・モデルです。

OHC4気筒 2.3ℓの堅実なエンジンを搭載。穏やかななかにも、ピリッとめりはりの効いた性能で、メルセデス・ベンツの味を一番お手近に味わっていただける5人乗りセダンですむろん4速トルコン自動ミッションをはじめ、各種パワー装潢を標準装備。インテリアは美しいファブリック張りです

NEW COMPACT SEDAN 240D

経済的な高級乗用車 4気筒のディーゼル・セダンです。

燃料費がごく僅かで済む上、丈夫で長持ち。しかもガソリン車なみのスムーズさを併せ持っているのが、この4気筒 2.4ℓ予燃焼室式ディーゼル・エンジンを搭載した240Dです。トランスミッションは4速マニュアルまたは4速トルコン[※]が選べ、各種パワー装潢も標準装備のハイグレードな5人乗りセダンです（写真は欧州仕様車です）

Section of the first Yanase (the main Japanese distributor) catalogue to feature the W123 models.

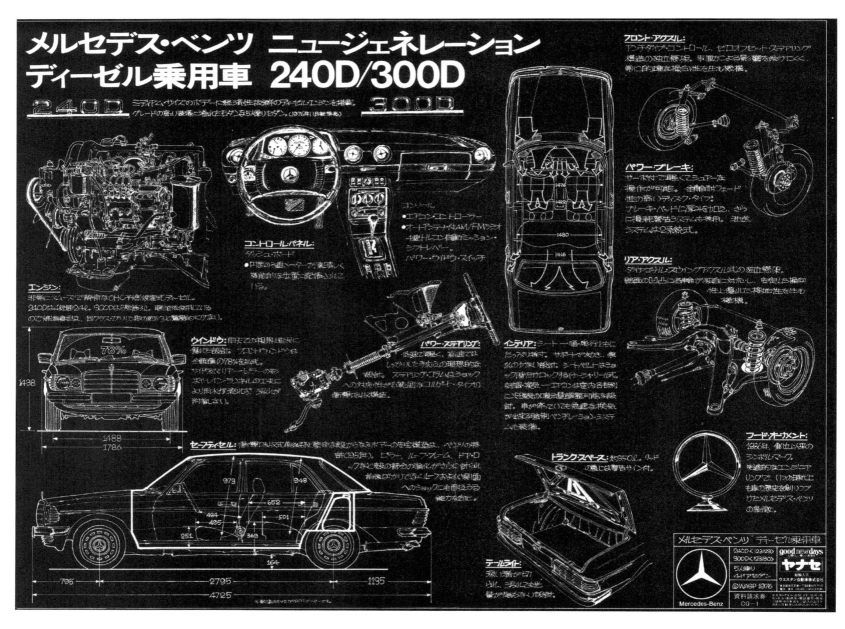

Japanese advertising from early 1977.

W123 production

This fascinating series of shots was taken at the Sindelfingen plant in early 1977. We can see the front suspension being installed, a halogen light unit being fitted (note the 'H4' marking on the lens and the extended rubber dressing piece below the light), a dashboard going in and more being prepared as cars float by above, a steering wheel being secured, completed vehicles being checked over, and W123 and W116 models about to be delivered.

The special chassis model

Before moving on, it should be noted that the first batch of special chassis versions of the W123 series was released in July 1976. This range of partial-bodied variants allowed coachbuilders such as Binz of Lorch, Miesen of Bonn, Rappold of Wülfrath, Pollman of Bremen, Welsch of Mayen and Stolle of Hanover to display their skills by converting the W123 into all manner of specialized vehicles, from hearses to ambulances, and even the odd pick-up truck.

They were basically regular cars from the front to the B-post, and then the back was left open and untrimmed so that fresh bodywork could be created with ease. The back doors and C-posts were left in place on standard wheelbase cars, but the fuel tank was moved to the side to allow a flat bed over the rear axle, the spare wheel deleted, and there was no rear lighting whatsoever, as there was nothing there in the way of metalwork on which to mount the combination lights. The long-wheelbase versions were very much the same, but the B-post area was cut and shut after an extra 630mm (24.8in) of suitably stiffened structure was added in-between the separated halves. Incidentally, the special chassis vehicles left the factory on 15in steel wheels and tyres, instead of the usual 14in rims specified on the standard saloons.

Initially, there was the 230 at DM 19,114, a 250 long-wheelbase version at DM 25,940, a pair of 240Ds (one standard wheelbase at DM 20,191, plus a lwb one at DM 24,242), and a 300D lwb version at DM 25,841. From late-1977, a few

The standard wheelbase special-purpose chassis as it was shipped from the Daimler-Benz works.

The long-wheelbase version of the special-purpose chassis.

An ambulance by Binz, created on the swb chassis.

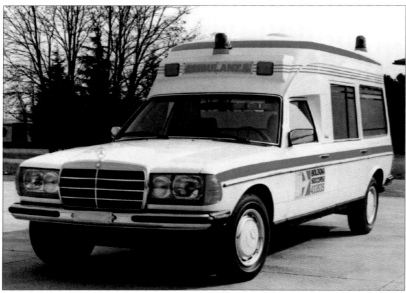

One of the 280E lwb special-purpose chassis models, seen here converted into an ambulance by the Grazia concern of Italy.

The Bremen plant belonging to Daimler-Benz, pictured here in 1978.

A hearse by Pollman, based on the 250 lwb chassis.

European export countries were allowed to import a 280E long-wheelbase chassis, too, which was perfect for high-speed ambulance applications, but never sold in Germany.

Dr Wilfried Guth (an ex-Deutsche Bank man) was at the helm of the Supervisory Board by now, and one of his first decisions was to make the forthcoming estate version of the W123 at the Bremen plant – first established by Borgward in 1938, but inherited by Daimler-Benz after the Hanomag takeover. This gradual move from commercial vehicle to passenger car production would duly become significant for fans of Mercedes sports cars at the end of the 1980s, and certainly increased production volume at a time when the Sindelfingen plant was bursting at the seams and still couldn't keep up with demand for the W123 models.

The estate – or station wagon – was only one new variation to add to the W123 line-up, though. In addition to the saloon and special chassis version covered so far, the 123 series range would be expanded by the aforementioned estate, a two-door coupé, and a long-wheelbase saloon for trade users. With the multitude of engine and gearbox options available, plus all these body variations, things became very complicated very quickly, even before export markets were considered. The next chapter treads gently in what is truly a minefield of epic proportions …

5

Mid-life offshoots

The Stuttgart company had invested a lot of time and money in the process of getting the W123 off the ground, not only in terms of tying up engineers and designers and the traditional costs one expects when developing a new car, but also a huge level of investment in new plant equipment. In order to recoup this outlay at a faster pace, high-volume sales were needed, and the Mercedes marketing men had a field day exploring different variations that could be produced on a limited budget to widen the appeal of the W123 series. The special chassis models were looked at briefly in the previous chapter, while this one introduces the two- and five-door machines, along with the lwb cars that augmented the ever-popular saloon line-up ...

Selected members of the press had been given a sneak preview of the coupé (duly dubbed the C123) alongside the saloons at the time of their launch. There was no secret made of its existence, so its appearance as a production model was hardly a shock. In fact, with the 'Stroke Eight' coupés' success to build on, planning for the two-door model had started as far back as April 1972.

The two-door model's design work was conducted under Friedrich Geiger, and one can see the master's touch translated in the metalwork from a number of his design sketches made during the '/8' era. By this time, of course, most of the W123 saloon's styling – on which the C123 would be based – was already in place, so once the 85mm (3.3in) shorter wheelbase had been confirmed, it was only really the roof section that offered designers any room for manoeuvre. Some early proposals hinted at a Targa-style roof, albeit a fake one, while others looked to the past for inspiration (with a taste of the old 'Fintail' coupés and late W121 and W198 II SL hardtops shining through) or borrowed from the C107 SLC's elegant styling.

Ultimately, the transformation from saloon to coupé was a very simple one, with the final design being visible in full-size models built as early as September 1973. As with the saloon, a few details still needed ironing out, but the end was clearly

The W123 saloon was about to be joined by some interesting variations on a theme ...

An early design proposal with Targa-style embellishment.

This picture from September 1973 shows a full-size model awaiting styling review. Note the use of the 'W123C' moniker at this stage (rather than 'C123'), and the '250C' badge on the tail.

A clay model being prepared for the C123 project.

Elegant roofline and window graphics of the coupé.

in sight. For the record, Geiger retired in December 1973, eventually handing the reins to Bruno Sacco, who would serve the company well for many years, ultimately as head of styling – a position that oversaw a growing number of Chief Designers as the Mercedes model range evolved and expanded.

Although the height was reduced by 43mm (1.7in), the C123's heavily-strengthened roof was actually quite similar to the saloon one, with the rain channel extended across the small rear side window and then folded downwards in a similar fashion to the four-door car. This chrome trim was heavier on the two-door model, though, aping that of the C107 by joining a heavy

vertical chrome trim piece added below the side glass to give the impression of a gentle downward sweep from the C- to the B-post that then swept upward towards the door mirror area. This added interest to the window graphics, which were decidedly plain on the saloon.

Other features included a pillarless side window design, a plain C-post (it will be remembered that the saloons had a dressing piece at the base of the pillar), and a more stylish rear window that was closer to the SLC in looks than the W123 saloon. Getting the pillarless windows right took a great deal of work, as Jaguar soon found out when developing the XJ6C,

The clever packaging meant the C123 was every bit as practical as the W123 on which it was based. The only sacrifice was some legroom and headroom in the rear.

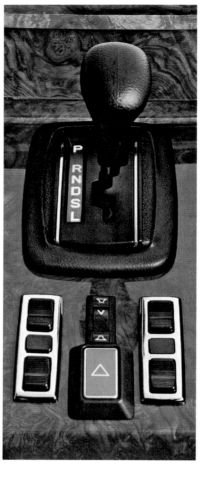

The tasteful walnut trim used on the early cars.

but the narrow chrome strip separating the two windows looked supremely balanced, and as well as providing a guard against wind noise and the weather, added strength to the rear side window when the front window was lowered: when both side windows were down, the chrome piece moved with the rear pane, leaving the entire flank of the vehicle open to the elements. The coupés also came with the headlights, bumpers, bulkhead grille trim, and rear light protectors found on the 2.8-litre saloons, adding more class and chrome into the equation. All told, through a combination of subtle styling changes and low-profile tyres for all two-door variants, the C123 looked lower, longer, and an awful lot sportier than its W123 stablemate – an impression that was backed up by some tuning of the rear suspension components to enhance handling without compromising ride quality.

Moving inside, the front seats (still upholstered in cloth as standard, but coming with height adjustment on all coupé grades) gained a vacuum-controlled tilt and locking device on the backrest to allow access to the rear of the car, releasing whenever a door was opened, a more luxurious rear bench seat with a heavy central armrest and removable centre section that revealed a storage box, revised door trim to the sides of it to allow for the shorter panel and seatbelt turret in the B-post area, and an ashtray added in the centre of its base. Manual window lifts were considered the norm, but power-assisted steering and central locking was classed as standard, and the interior was brightened up no end by the application of walnut veneer-style trim pieces on the dashboard and centre console.

However, with the work required to get the W123 saloons off the ground and other pressing projects, it soon became clear

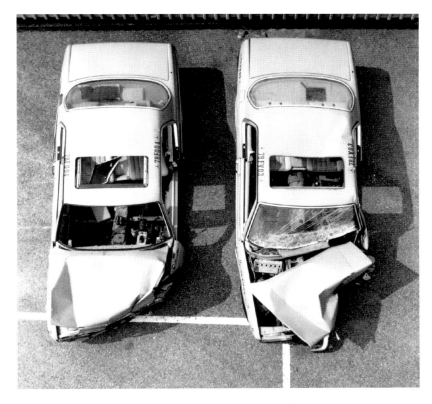

The coupé underwent the same ongoing safety programme as the saloons. According to the car numbers, these crash tests were carried out in 1978.

scale production of the two-door models starting in April (or June for the 230C), and duly employed on the 250, 280 and 280E saloons as well, but not the 230 sedan, hence the use of 'basically' in the second sentence of this paragraph. The four-speed G76/18D came with subtly different internal ratios to the 18B and 18C versions, having a 3.98 cog on first, 2.29 on second, 1.45 on third, and a direct top; the final-drive ratios were unchanged at this point, although the four 2.8-litre cars inherited a 3.58:1 back axle in November 1977. The four-speed W4B025 automatic option continued as before, duly gaining the revised final-drive ratio employed on 4MT cars at the end of the year.

Of the three models sold in the domestic marketplace, the Americans received only the 280CE, arriving Stateside just in time for the 1978 Model Year. However, US buyers had the chance to order the unique 300CD coupé – a two-door model (code 123.150) powered by the 3-litre diesel engine. Pilot production began in May 1977, with full-scale production beginning four months later, although the at-odds image of a sporting CI machine – much less a luxury sporting one – and the distinct lack of infrastructure to deal with private diesel car users in the States at the time meant this was something of a brave move for Daimler-Benz and its MBNA partners, put forward in a bid to deal with CAFE (corporate average fuel economy) requirements without downsizing its range.

Continued page 94

that a spring 1976 launch date – as originally planned – was out of the question. In the end, the car's official announcement came in September 1976, with the pilot build taking place in the following month to allow for a proper press launch in the New Year. The C123 then made its public debut at the 1977 Geneva Show, which ran from 17-27 March that particular year …

The coupé in the marketplace

In Germany, the two-door C123 line-up consisted of three models – the 230C (type number 123.043), priced at DM 25,064, the 280C (123.050) at DM 29,848, and the 280CE (123.053) at DM 31,835. The powertrains were basically carried over from the equivalent saloons, with only minor differences – such as a revised exhaust system – required to suit the coupé's tighter packaging. In addition, all coupés sported the G76/18D (716.006) manual gearbox, introduced to coincide with the full-

The three early coupé variants circulating the test track at Untertürkheim.

91

Left and opposite: Various views of the home market 230C two-door model. In reality, one needed to see the badge on the tail of the coupés to tell which grade was which.

93

Stunning photography from the first coupé catalogue. It was later retouched when the 280C fell by the wayside.

Both US-bound coupés came with an automatic transmission only, but were fully-loaded, with tinted glass, air-conditioning, PAS, cruise control, central locking, power windows and a stereo radio all classed as part of the package. An interesting addition on the 300CD, along with other CI models, was a huge directory of diesel service stations – a sign of the times, especially as most listed were truck stops at this stage.

Following a cross-country test of the 300CD, *Motor Trend* wrote: "It would seem that an energetic squirrel in a roller cage would do as well for propulsion, until it is understood that a diesel runs at its most efficient at or near peak power. Perhaps the most interesting thing about the Mercedes 300 diesel is that it is now civilized. There is no special drill to go through to start and stop it. For the most part, you are hardly aware that it's a diesel.

An early pre-production coupé on the move. This picture turned up in catalogues for many years.

"If we were to be asked at this point whether we would opt for the 280CE or 300CD, our reply would have to be that it depended on where we lived. If we lived in relatively flat country, the cost-per-mile factor would be a strong point in favour of the diesel. The thing is trouble-free, it is dead reliable, it doesn't require tune-ups, it will likely last forever, and it costs less than your average econobox to drive. These are pretty strong arguments in favour of the 300CD."

Rather than location, and despite the country's low speed limits, the majority of buyers would base their purchase decision on performance, of course; someone with the required $20,000 budget to join the coupé club would hardly be worried about a few cents here and there on petrol costs. While the 280CE was no ball of fire in US-spec, clocking up a 19.2 second standing-quarter time with *Car & Driver*, the 1590kg (3495lb) 300CD was three seconds and a full 12mph (19kph) slower as it passed the quarter-mile marker.

Another early European-spec coupé, this one fitted with alloy wheels. Oddly, the coupé was less aerodynamic than the saloon, coming with a Cd figure of 0.43. This can be attributed to the shorter roof section.

Amongst the right-hand drive markets, just as the 1978 season was dawning, the UK received the 230C in October 1977, priced at £8950 including taxes, and the 280CE, which commanded almost £11,000. Both came with an automatic gearbox as standard, but add in extras like alloy wheels (£519), power windows (£207), a power roof (£363), and even basic things like seatbelts (£35) and the coupé became a very expensive commodity.

The 230C suffered from the same problem as the diesel model in America – 109 horses have to work hard to propel a car that officially tipped the scales at 1375kg (3025lb), but was a good 200kg (440kg) heavier in reality. Thankfully, the EU-spec engines were livelier, with the 230C matching the quarter-mile time of the US-spec 280CE; but the little Benz was still painfully slow compared with most of its rivals – beaten even by middleweights like the Opel Commodore GSE, let alone the Jaguars and BMWs.

Summing up the 230C, *Motor* concluded: "The 230C is an excellent car in many areas where Mercedes traditionally reign supreme – the sheer integrity of its engineering, the high standard of assembly, its safety and impeccable road manners. It is also stylish and fairly exclusive – features valued by many buyers. But the fact remains that it is slow and cramped compared to the sort of cars that are available for the same money. Looked at objectively, it seems very poor value, yet we have a sneaking suspicion that looks and exclusivity alone will enable Mercedes to sell as many coupés as they want."

Further afield, the Australian and Japanese markets eventually got the 280CE in spring 1978 – the only model to make it across the seas to these rhd outlets. Actually, it should be mentioned here, that just as many lhd cars were sold in Japan as rhd machines, for Japanese buyers tend to love the kudos attached to a left-hooker – a steering wheel on the wrong side screams 'import car' and the bragging rights that come with it. Strange, but true.

Meanwhile

With the 123 series an assured success, a few minor changes were applied to ease production and improve the car's detailing. During April 1977, the centre console became a push-fit item rather than being screwed into place, and a multi-layer mat was

A W123 saloon built during mid-1977, as it has the heavier C-post trim but earlier-style sill guards. Note the fairing over the sunroof; similar items were available as a dealer accessory for the side windows, too.

used instead of bitumen to give better noise insulation in the front floorpan area. At the same time, a new tufted carpet material was phased in on all models, and the decorative strip on the rear pillar of the saloons was revised, becoming a fraction heavier than before, especially on the leading edge. We've already noted the gearbox change on the sixes and the 230C, so no need to say any more on that subject.

May saw the adoption of improved diffuser lenses on the headlights, and June brought with it a slightly slower ratio on the PAS system – the new 16.5:1 ratio giving 3.2 turns lock-to-lock, whereas the old 14.2 ratio gave 2.7 turns. This change was adopted on all cars fitted with power-assisted steering, and came just in time for the start of 230C production. On the subject of coupés, the front seats on the two-door models were modified to improve headroom, while July saw a stronger 55A alternator specified on M115-engined machines, matching that of the six-cylinder cars (the earlier unit had been rated at a significantly lower 35A).

The 123 series gained some more enhancements in August, with improved noise insulation, a second horn added for all cars, and a warning device to inform the driver that lights had been left on or a door was ajar.

In other news, at the end of 1977, an all-alloy V8 was introduced on the 450SLC 5.0, while at the other end of the scale, in view of the US CAFE mandate and proposed gas guzzler taxes, a turbo-diesel engine was launched for the 300SD saloon. On 14 October that year, the 5,000,000th postwar passenger car left the line at Sindelfingen. Interestingly, the first million cars built after the conflict had taken 16 years to complete, whilst this last batch of a million had taken just two years. A few weeks later, Hans Scherenberg retired, leaving Werner Breitschwerdt in charge of product development.

The lwb cars

In September 1977, the 240D Lang model (type 123.125) was added to the 123 series line-up at DM 33,100, along with the 300D Lang (123.132) at DM 34,699, and 250 Lang (123.028) at DM 34,798. Rather than traditional long-wheelbase luxury models that simply allowed a little extra legroom in the rear for executives and VIP types, these particular lwb machines,

The long-wheelbase car compared to the standard saloon. The extended cars were real heavyweights, tipping the scales at between 1540kg (3388lb) and 1615kg (3553lb), depending on the engine.

A lwb model in service. Most were bought by private hire firms.

designated V123s, were aimed more at commercial users, such as high-class taxi firms, undertakers, and so on.

The styling was essentially the same as the regular saloons, but with the rear door squared off on the trailing edge, and C-pillar area extended forwards to fill up the gap created by the significantly longer 3425mm (134.8in) wheelbase. To balance this from a styling point of view and help carry the extra weight, the lwb cars rode on a 15in wheel and tyre combination. Inside, a folding centre row of seats (split so as to give seating for one, two or three people) was added to justify the car's additional length, leading to a 7/8-seater vehicle classification. It was quite

an elegant conversion, helping to further extend the 123 series range with minimal investment.

The 1978 model year

A new price list was issued in Germany in January 1978, with the 123 series line-up already extending to no fewer than 15 models. The prices were as follows: DM 19,196 for the 200 saloon; the 230 saloon DM 20,160; the 250 saloon DM 22,960; the 250 lwb model DM 35,112; the 280 saloon DM 26,365; the 280E saloon DM 28,370; the 200D saloon DM 19,712; the 220D saloon DM 20,530; the 240D saloon

The diesel-powered C111-III (right) picked up a number of world speed records in April 1978, building on those established by the C111-IID next to it in 1976. The W123 saloon dates from 1977, but the diesel engine link is the key point.

DM 21,246; the 240D lwb model DM 33,398; the 300D saloon DM 23,531; the 300D lwb model DM 35,011; the 230C coupé DM 25,290; the 280C coupé DM 30,117; and the 280CE coupé DM 32,122.

More production changes were applied to the 123 series in general. The 300D-based cars gained a stronger 55A alternator (previously 35A) in September 1977, with the four-cylinder diesels following suit soon after, complete with uprated starter motors; the PAS system alignment

was revised slightly, and the rocker switches found on the dashboard were given a subtly chamfered edge. A couple of weeks later, a new steering rack was used on vehicles without PAS, the trim strips just above the sills were made larger to cover the lowermost section of the door, the heating was improved (a backlit symbol plate for the heater controls was duly adopted in December), and a key-type starter system – like that found on the 300D – was fitted to the 240D model.

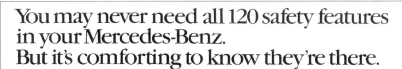

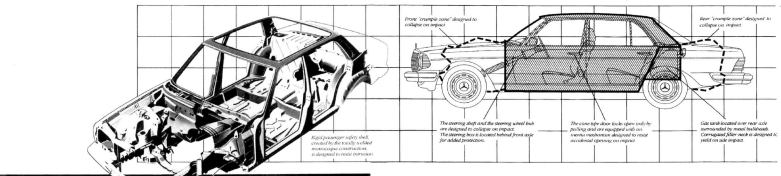

You may never need all 120 safety features in your Mercedes-Benz. But it's comforting to know they're there.

Of the 120 safety features built as standard equipment into every new Mercedes-Benz, those designed to meet U.S. safety standards represent less than half. Those designed to meet Mercedes-Benz safety standards represent the rest.

The washboard principle

For instance, the engineers wanted to keep the car's taillights visible in foul weather. Solution: taillight lenses ribbed like washboards. Wind tunnel tests showed that most dirt and slush tend to collect on the outer surfaces – leaving the recessed grooves cleaner, longer.

Because a side impact *might* activate a push button and this in turn might pop open a door, the engineers designed push buttons out of the door handles of a Mercedes-Benz. They will open only by pulling.

The engineers even found a way to make the mouldings that frame the windshield work in the cause of safety.

They are actually designed to deflect rainwater away from the side windows as you cruise along in the wet.

The windshield wipers, on the other hand, are aerodynamically designed to sweep across the windshield

Electric sunroof (shown) available at added cost.

with the airflow and thus resist "lifting," even in high-speed turbulence.

Seeing is surviving

Mercedes-Benz takes a dim view of styling that obstructs driver visibility; you can't avoid what you can't see. Result: a Mercedes-Benz driver is surrounded by as much glass as possible – in the sedans, for example, by a sweep of 85 percent unobstructed visibility.

Notice that the fuel filler flap of a Mercedes-Benz is placed far ahead on the right rear fender, almost above the wheel. No random act: it leads to a fuel tank mounted so deep inboard that it sits above the rear axle – as far from exposure to a rear-end impact as possible.

Strong law, stronger locks

You may be heartened to know that the door locks on a Mercedes-Benz conform not just to the letter of the law but to its spirit. They far *exceed* the strength demanded by U.S. federal law.

No law dictates it, but "crumple zones" at the front and rear of a Mercedes-Benz body are designed to yield accordion-like, to absorb kinetic energy in a heavy impact and

lessen its effect on the passenger compartment.

The steering box in a Mercedes-Benz sits *behind* the front axle, for extra protection. The steering column is designed to yield and collapse on impact. The steering wheel itself is deformable and its flat, padded center is meant to help dissipate the effect of a heavy impact over a large area.

Every new Mercedes-Benz is safety-padded in the usual places, plus some unusual ones: e.g., the underside of the instrument panel and the knob of the shift lever. The engineers didn't want the glove-box door to pop open on an impact and become a menace to the front seat passenger – so the lock on the glove-box door isn't a push button but a *sliding* mechanism.

The search goes on

These are some examples of the 120 safety features built into every new Mercedes-Benz. Imposing as that number may seem, it is by no means a final one. Safety research and development at Mercedes-Benz have not stopped – and it is intended that they never will.

© 1978 Mercedes-Benz of North America, Inc. One Mercedes Drive, Montvale, N.J. 07645

American advertising from 1978, zooming in on safety aspects.

December 1977 saw the general availability of the signature Fuchs alloy wheels, which had been slow in coming through due to a production hold-up, along with the option of a 30mm (1.2in) lower front seat for the coupés. After the Christmas break, the manual sunroof was revised, and the seatbelt operation further optimized.

The various Becker stereo units were revised over the autumn 1977 to spring 1978 period, with the 'Grand Prix' stereo radio gaining more buttons and different control knobs, although the SA 516 option code was retained all the way through until the unit was dropped in December 1982. The 'Mexico' radio/cassette gained an auto-reverse feature, but again retained the old SA 511 code as far as Daimler-Benz was concerned, and stayed as an option until October 1980. And then there were the two 'Europa' variants, which inherited the same styling changes as the 'Grand Prix' unit. Both kept their old SA 514 and 257 codes, with the former staying on the option list until April 1983, and the latter continuing all the way through to the end of W123 production, gaining rubber control knobs in the last year or so of its run. Finally, from September 1977 to December 1980, dealers offered a basic traffic news radio using the SA 259 option code; finding one today would be a real rarity.

Automatic air-conditioning became available for the M110-engined cars in the spring, but not on those fitted with auxiliary heating (the latter, ordered via option code SA 228, featured a different glovebox arrangement to allow for the fitment of the timing system). The door locks were modified on the coupés at the same time.

Following the change from the 110.984 to the 110.988 engine in the European 280E models (with an increase in the c/r, larger exhaust valves, new inlet and exhaust manifolds and a different air cleaner bringing about an improvement of 8bhp), domestic prices were revised again in April 1978, with an across-the-board rise of around 3.5 per cent, taking the entry-level model up to DM 19,858 and the flagship of the coupé line up to DM 33,342. At the same time, five estate models were added to the list, but more on these later …

In the export markets, the 240D and 300D saloons had accounted for very nearly half of MBNA's record sales figure of 48,872 units over 1977. For 1978, they were priced at $12,762

(POE) and $17,798, respectively, while the two-door 300CD commanded $19,987. The 230 was gone by now, leaving two 2.8-litre cars in the petrol line-up – the $18,348 280E and the $20,610 280CE. The contemporary S-Class models ranged from $21,687 to $41,444 at this time, although cheaper but competent competitors were everywhere – for example, the $7145 Volvo 244DL from Sweden, the $17,500 Jaguar XJ6 (even the XJ12 was only $19,200!) from England, and the $14,195 BMW 530 from Mercedes' homeland.

Prices in the UK were flying upwards at a rate of knots, with around £1000 being added to the 123 series, and this at a time when one could buy cars like the Mini 850, Toyota 1000 or Simca 1000LS for less than £2000. Notwithstanding, for 1978, the Mercedes 200 saloon was listed at £5995 including taxes, with the 200D at £6250, the 230 and 240D at £7594, the 250 at £8395, the 230C at £8951, the 300D at £8995, the 280E at £9695, and 280CE at £10,990; the last four models came with an automatic gearbox as standard. For the record, the flagship of the UK range was the 450SEL 6.9, which commanded a hefty

The UK distributors had the same thing in mind, and at the same time, too.

Crayford Conversions launched its rare and desirable 'St Tropez' convertible in 1978. Based on the 280CE and featuring a power hood, the transformation cost the same kind of money as a 200 saloon!

£23,851 – enough to buy three 3.5-litre SD1 Rovers and still have enough change for a Vanden Plas 1500! At least seatbelts were standard by now, but in response to climbing prices, PAS was moved to the option list on the manual-only 200 and 200D grades in July 1978, costing an extra £259, while, to rub salt into the wound, the base cars were around £350 to £450 more than at the start of the year.

The British weekly *Autocar* tried a 200 saloon for size, and after clocking a sluggish 0-60 time of 15.3 seconds, a top speed of 96mph (155kph) and a pleasing average fuel consumption of 22.1mpg, declared: "If you take performance, economy, space and handling only into consideration, and forget price for a moment, then the Mercedes is bettered by many of its rivals. Take the price into consideration, and it seems a terribly expensive car which certainly has the looks of the 'traditional' Mercedes with little of the glamour and performance."

Motor Sport managed to get its hands on an automatic 280CE, and declared: "Now that Jaguar have ceased production of XJ coupés, Mercedes have a niche all to themselves in this section of the quality market with this elegant, superbly engineered coupé. A splendid car."

The 240D model had been added to the Australian line-up as the 1977 season progressed, costing $23,455 in automatic guise. However, there was a big price increase for the 1978 season, taking the newcomer up $1000, but other models up much further. Indeed, the 240D became the cheapest car in the 123 series range at this stage, with the 230 now costing $26,500 for 1978, and the top-of-the-line 280E a hefty $31,300. As a small consolation, at least the uprated 280E, released in the spring, continued with the same sticker price, while the 280CE coupé made its debut at the same time, priced at $40,700 – roughly the same as a V12 Jaguar XJ-S.

The Japanese market had settled down by now as well, with the '/8' series finally out of the way. The 240D was the cheapest car in the armoury, priced at ¥4,720,000 in manual guise, or ¥5,275,000 as an automatic. All other models came with a 4AT gearbox only, with the 230 at ¥5,520,000, 300D at ¥5,970,000, and the 280E at ¥6,986,000 as a saloon, or about 15 per cent more as a coupé after its launch at the tail-end of spring. To put these prices in perspective, the contemporary automatic Volvo 244DL commanded ¥4,190,000.

The S123 estate

Based on the same wheelbase as the saloons, the patent for the design of the estate rests with Bruno Sacco (the new Chief Designer) and Joseph Gallitzendörfer, who had played an influential role in shaping a number of classic Mercedes-Benz models since the mid-1960s, which is when he left the Rosenthal ceramics firm to join the styling department in Stuttgart. However, the panelwork from the B-post forward was taken directly from the W123 saloon. To keep costs in check, and with the same distance between the wheels and the brief to keep the same overall length as well, styling options were fairly restricted – about the only real variations one can see in the earlier design proposals from 1973 are in rooflines and window graphics, although a few oddball wing extensions were looked at and quickly dismissed.

By October 1974, the design was ready enough to be presented to the Board of Management for approval – not to be signed off at this stage, simply approved as a production-worthy project, which is something that was duly achieved. Ironically, the 1974 prototype was closer to the showroom model than some of the later styling bucks, some of which tried to retain a

Bruno Sacco, seen here with a scale model of the SEC.

One of several full-size styling bucks for the S123 estate, this one pictured in October 1974.

The main selling point of the estate was the versatility afforded to it by the large cargo area, which could easily be transformed around seating requirements. The low floor and wide space between the rear light units made the car extremely practical.

semblance of the saloon's tail, while others sported different rear combination lights that looked better but often cut into the width of the loading area, making the idea impractical.

Signed off as a production model at the end of September 1975, yet still not christened the T-Modell until April 1977, the estate featured a reinforced floorpan at the rear, new rear doors with a sharper trailing edge at the top, a new roof, and C-pillar area with additional side windows to suit the wide, top-

hinged one-piece tailgate arrangement (with standard wash/wipe and a heated rear screen), and the pair of gas struts that held it in place when open, and revised rear light units, with a single reversing light and foglight dropped onto bumper blade. Following saloon practice, the upmarket 280TE version featured different headlights and chrome grilles on the bulkhead to make it stand out from lesser grades (although, oddly, the bumpers were shared across all grades on the estates), while the chrome

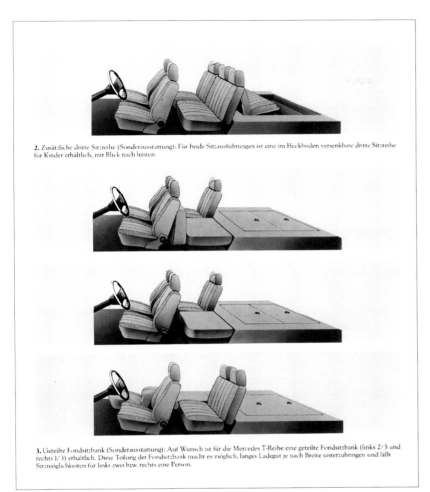

2. Zusätzliche dritte Sitzreihe (Sonderausstattung): Für beide Sitzausführungen ist eine im Heckboden versenkbare dritte Sitzreihe für Kinder erhältlich, mit Blick nach hinten.

3. Geteilte Fondsitzbank (Sonderausstattung): Auf Wunsch ist für die Mercedes T-Reihe eine geteilte Fondsitzbank (links 2/3 und rechts 1/3) erhältlich. Diese Teilung der Fondsitzbank macht es möglich, langes Ladegut je nach Breite unterzubringen und läßt Sitzmöglichkeiten für links zwei bzw. rechts eine Person.

The seating arrangement options with the split rear seat and third row bench – both extras, but probably well worth the investment. The standard rear bench seat folded in a similar fashion to the split one, ie the lower cushion folded forward on its front hinges, while the backrest folded forward on its rear hinges. The cushion section was removable if required, allowing the front seat to fully tilt back.

roof-rails, made standard for all S123s during July 1978, could be readily converted into a roof-rack; aerodynamic top boxes, ski racks and so on could be specified as an option to suit, or the SA 725 code deleted the roof bars if the owner preferred. Tinted glass was available, by the way, ordered via the SA 599 code.

Mechanically, apart from a relocated fuel tank (further forward and under the floor) and spare tyre (tucked up on the nearside aft of the rear wheel, with the toolkit, folding warning triangle

and first aid box on the opposite side, behind the trim panel), the estates were pretty much identical to the equivalent saloons, although the rear suspension sported the hydropneumatic self-levelling set-up that was optional on the other 123 series cars, the slave cylinders were enlarged on the rear brakes, and the 230T and 250T came with the wider wheels and tyres fitted to the 230C; there was also a heavy-load upgrade available that came with a larger brake servo and 15in wheels and tyres (option code SA 912). There were no surprises inside the car either, other than an optional split rear seat (SA 843) that came with a 1:3/2:3 folding facility to allow longer loads to be combined with seating, and the option of a folding rearward-facing bench seat in the luggage area (SA 844), the latter cleverly leaving a flat floor when it was stored away, as per the regular back seats. Unique interior options included things like a retractable luggage cover (SA 541) and auxiliary heating (SA 229) for the back, a set of three headrests (SA 431), and load anchorage points (SA 724), the latter being available from the summer of 1979; things like dog guards were available as accessories from dealers.

Previewed at the 1977 Frankfurt Show, the estate (or station wagon, although the Benz marketing men preferred to call it the T-Modell) was the last major variant on the 123 series theme,

Estate production at the Bremen plant, with a 280TE in the foreground.

Flashback to the 1978 Geneva Show. The same circular stand as that used in Frankfurt a few months earlier for the S123 preview was called up for duty again, although the 1977 exhibit had roof rails only rather than rails and top boxes.

with the pilot build having begun as early as September 1977 to allow for full-scale production (scheduled for 24,000 units a year) in Hall 3 at the Bremen plant from early-April 1978 onwards. Initially, five grades were made available, with the vehicle's added kerb weight and load-carrying capacity ruling out the smaller engine options, despite the estates having a fractionally better 0.41 Cd figure. In Germany, the 230T was introduced at DM 25,290 during the spring, with the 250T at DM 27,854, the 280TE at DM 33,757, the 240TD at DM 26,421, and the 300TD at DM 28,784.

A couple of months after the estates started drifting into showrooms, the bonnet catch mechanism was improved on all 123 series cars, and the oil cooler deleted on the 240D. Then, in July 1978, power-assisted steering was made standard on the 240D and 240TD models. Bigger changes were in store for the 1979 season, though …

The 1979 model year

Most of the domestic prices were carried over for the 1979 season, with only the 250 saloon, 240D models, and the five estates suffering cost increases in the August 1978 listing. The 250s gained PAS as standard, accounting for the DM 695 rise, the 240Ds had a DM 336 premium added due to engine modifications, and all the estates had DM 235 added because roof-rails and the rack system had become standard. On some models, of course, such as the 250T, one needed to add two new items together, meaning an increase of DM 930 on that particular grade, but otherwise prices held steady for a few months.

As it happens, both the 240D and 300D engines had been modified in August 1978, but somehow the 3-litre cars had escaped the eye of the accountants, despite receiving a similar level of revisions. Oddly, neither engine was given a new code number, but the OM616 D24 had its bore adjusted by 0.1mm to take the displacement down from 2404cc to 2399cc, while the OM617 D30 unit got the same change to take the five's cubic capacity down from 3005cc to 2998cc. Only the 2.4-litre engine had any leading specification changes as a result, though, with power going up from 65bhp to 72bhp thanks to a few minor tweaks to the valvetrain, combustion chambers and an improved exhaust system.

There were more changes made to the Becker stereos in September 1978, with the pair of 'Monza' cassette player variants gaining a few revisions, although the SA 510 and 258 codes were carried over, and both only lasted in the catalogues until August 1979 anyway. A new, rather attractive 'Europa' cassette player was offered alongside the updated Monzas, but both were to be short-lived, lasting until March 1980 when revised units took their place. Both carried the SA 512 and 254 codes of their predecessors, but by 1982, both had been revised, and they gained some further changes for 1985, when they continued alongside the long-running SA 257 unit.

Other changes at the start of the 1979 season included a larger receiver for the front seatbelts, a fresh accelerator pedal design with a new hinge, and a larger brake servo for all cars except the 200D and 220D models. And by November, cars were being fitted with a stud rather than a mushroom button on the door capping as an anti-theft measure, although it would be a while before this feature was seen in catalogue pictures – as with the majority of motor manufacturers, those who are commissioned to produce promotional material rarely keep up-to-date with changes filtering through, unless they are too obvious not to deal with them. Sometimes, even then they get ignored!

Domestic advertising announcing the arrival of the estate.

A 1979 saloon contending with German city traffic.

Prices in Germany rose by two per cent in December 1978 (caused by German law requiring the fitting of rear seatbelts in 1979, although one didn't have to use them until the law making their use compulsory was applied in 1984!), and then in February 1979, the cost of 200D motoring increased to DM 21,347 to cover the engine revisions applied to that model, along with the extra expense from gaining the key-starter system, the 88Ah battery already standard on the other diesels, and the larger brake servo fitted to the rest of the 123 series cars a few months earlier. The most

important thing, of course, was the 5bhp power increase, making the 200D strong enough to make the 220D redundant, and by the following month, the 2.2-litre diesel model had disappeared.

Other changes were applied in February 1979, including a modified automatic transmission for the 200D, 240D and 240TD models, although they didn't justify new type numbers or change the leading specifications. There was also a heavier steering lock for all cars (as well as a minor change to the steering mechanism), and a revised engine oil cooler design. Diesel models with air-

Beautiful image from the 1979 estate catalogue. Generally speaking, the station wagons weighed about 120kg (264lb) more than the equivalent saloon.

As it happens, there was another increase of about one per cent on domestic prices in July, but a second price list issued that month made the original out-of-date in days. We shall therefore concentrate on the second one in the next section of this chapter …

As for the major export outlets, the 1979 Oil Crisis, rooted in the troubles in Iran during late 1978, again saw another boom in diesel power in the States, as the price of oil more than doubled. It was a major factor in the early eighties US recession, and did a lot of damage to the European motor industry, with cheaper, more economical cars from Japan gaining a strong foothold in EU markets. But Mercedes had an answer for the problems with a formidable Stateside diesel line-up – the only hurdle to conquer was finding enough buyers with the ready cash to deal with prices that were spiraling out of control due to exchange rate fluctuations.

Even though Karlfried Nordmann and his men at MBNA put even more emphasis on diesel, Americans received just one of the new estates – the 300TD, which hit the showrooms in March 1979 at $24,162. After a test of a US-spec car, *Motor Trend* noted: "The 300TD is a comely wagon. It is based on a wonderful automobile, the W123. Every nook and hidden compartment (of which there are two in the back) is stuffed full of prestige. It will

conditioning gained a new Delco compressor, and fully automatic air-conditioning became available for the diesel models, too.

In the background, Daimler-Benz had first toyed with ABS brake systems in 1970, but they ultimately became available in December 1978, eventually filtering down to the 123 series. Two months later, the long-running G-Wagen off-roader (Mercedes' answer to the Range Rover) was introduced, originally developed as a joint-project with Steyr-Daimler-Puch.

In May 1979, the price on the majority of the domestic 123 series range went up by DM 196, while the cost of the estates increased by varying amounts. The cost of the 230T rose by DM 375, the 240TD by DM 398, the 250T and 300TD by DM 443, and the 280TE by DM 543 – an increase that took the latter up to DM 34,535 and the 123 series flagship position if we exclude the specialist long-wheelbase models.

The 300TD in US-spec guise.

One of the saloons for the American market. The 1979 season was to be the last that US cars used all-white headlight units – yellow foglights were adopted for the 1980 Model Year.

be surprisingly economical in terms of fuel costs, and it will not be shockingly expensive."

The 3-litre station wagon was joined in the States by the 240D saloon at $14,601, the 300D saloon at $20,302, the 280E saloon at $21,688, the 300CD coupé at $22,931, and the 280CE coupé at $24,224, in a Mercedes range that topped out with the 6.9-litre SEL at a whopping $48,728; all came with an automatic gearbox, although the 240D could be bought with a manual transmission if required. The MBNA team was definitely doing something right, though, despite the seemingly odd model mix, for 1979 was another record year for sales. After a flat 1978, 52,820 cars found new owners during the 12 months of 1979, with two-thirds of them being diesel-powered.

In Britain, 1979 Model Year prices were about £600 up on what they were in summer, or, to put it another way, around £1000 up on the same time last year. The 200 and 200D were available with manual transmissions only, and PAS was an option, while all the other cars had the choice of 4MT and 4AT gearboxes (a no-cost option on all but the 240Ds, for which an extra £485 was asked) and all came with power-assisted steering as standard. The UK line-up consisted of the 200, 230, 250, 250

Cars at Sindelfingen about to be transported by rail before being loaded on ships to cross the Atlantic, en route for America.

The 1979 280CE for the US market.

lwb, 280E, 200D, 240D, 240D lwb and 300D saloons and 230C and 280CE coupés at the start of the season, while the estates augmented the range during the summer – first the £9795 240TD and £12,995 280TE, and then the automatic 250T, which split them on price.

Unlike America, estate cars were hardly common in the UK, and decidedly rare in the luxury sector for many years. A few conversions spring to mind, with 'shooting brake' bodies on Jaguars and Aston Martins, and Crayford was marketing a nice estate based on the W116 S-Class at the time of the T-Modell's launch. During the seventies, on the mass-production front, the big Volvos, Citroëns and Fords were perhaps closest in concept to the S123, but they were far cheaper – even in top-of-the-range Granada 2.8i Ghia form, the Ford estate was still only just over £9000, while one could buy two Citroën CX2400S Safari models for the price of the basic 280TE, and still have enough change for a very nice holiday on some exotic shore. Add in things like the optional alloy wheels (£380), metallic paint (£285), headlamp wash/wipe system (£159), a passenger-side door mirror (£34), two-tone horn (£67), cruise control (£147), air-conditioning (£954), power windows (£397), sunroof (£295 in manual guise, or £370 in electric form, and always a bit more on the estates), heated seats (£158), orthopaedic seats (£63), third-row seats (£310), fire extinguisher (£19) and stereo equipment (around £950 for a Becker Mexico unit installed with an automatic aerial and rear speakers), and the Benz became a very expensive proposition.

It was against this background that *Motor* declared the 280TE to be "probably the world's finest estate car and certainly the most expensive on the market. There are cheaper, larger estates, but none with the prestige, engineering quality and all-round excellence of the Mercedes." After recording a 0-60 time of 9.5 seconds and a 118mph (189kph) top speed, the car was praised for its "excellent performance and dynamic ability allied to functionality and versatility." The average fuel consumption of 19mpg was fairly good, too, on a par with the contemporary competition.

When Mercedes-Benz (UK) Limited put an automatic 280CE on the test fleet, all the major magazines in Britain were queuing up to try it, as early tests had been carried out with the 230C, and that was considered to struggle in the power-to-weight stakes.

The legend in your lifetime.
The Mercedes-Benz 280E combines superb styling with excellent engineering, outstanding performance, concern for safety and luxurious comfort. To find out more, come and talk to us.
COLMORE DEPOT LTD
Barbourne Road, Worcester.
Tel: 0905 28461

A British advert showing the 280E saloon.

A W123 saloon with France-specification lighting. It looks similar to the combination the Americans would be using for 1980, but halogen headlights were used in the European markets.

With 185bhp on tap, the 280CE was much more in keeping with the sporty image portrayed by the two-door body.

Autocar recorded a 0-60 time of 10.4 seconds – a speed blunted by 1540kg (3388lb) of kerb weight to shift through a four-speed automatic gearbox, but that extra cog paid dividends in terms of fuel consumption, which averaged 20.8mpg for the test. The magazine noted that the 280CE was "an excellent car to drive quickly, with a ride/handling compromise better than Mercedes have achieved to date. The engine is delightfully smooth and eager, but gearbox changes are less than ideally matched, albeit very smooth."

The 230C was still a nice motor in any company, though. Regarding the smaller-engined two-door model, *Thoroughbred & Classic Cars* noted: "Even from a distance, the Mercedes 230C exudes an impeccable pedigree. Longer acquaintance with the car confirms the sheer quality of Daimler-Benz AG engineering, the attention to detail, and the refinement."

The 1980 season

After a positive glut of new 123 series variants one after the other, the 1980 Model Year represented a chance for things to settle down now all the different body styles were in the showrooms and selling like hotcakes. However, rather than rest on its laurels, the Stuttgart company decided to take the opportunity to introduce a whole range of improvements that gave birth to the so-called 'Series 2' cars.

From September 1979, all cars received a fresh paint and trim line-up, along with new carpet material and a new grain pattern on moulded plastic parts. Interestingly, the black velour option was called just that – Black – whereas the earlier velour trim had been christened Anthracite, even though other trim materials in the same shade went by the Black name; oddly, when the 'Series 3' modifications came through, the velour trim only was given the Anthracite name again. To match the estates, the trim in the boot of the four-door and coupé models was improved, too, gaining carpet on the luggage compartment floor instead of rubber matting, and additional carpeting on the bulkhead between the boot and fuel tank.

In addition, a new steering wheel (similar to before but without the ribbing on the edges of the centre boss) and column surround was fitted, smaller headrests minus 'ears' were adopted, the pneumatic headlight range adjustment was moved to a thumb switch on the console above the HVAC controls, close to the driver, and there were fresh symbols and markings added on the group of three minor instruments (with symbols replacing wording) and the heater controls. At the same time, fully-automatic air-conditioning (option code SA 581) became

The 'Series 2' dashboard and fascia, with a new steering wheel, and symbols on the left-hand gauge beyond it. Note also the latest cloth trim pattern, which was easy to spot as being different to the earlier design; again, the 280s and coupés had their own pattern cloth, made up of oblong boxes, although it has to be said, it's a rare sight. M-B Tex and leather upholstery, however, looked very much the same as it did on the earlier cars, even though codes had changed (careful inspection reveals a slight difference in the perforations), and velour fabric was basically the same design.

110

and injection pump, plus new pistons, injector nozzles and glowplugs. The same 617.912 engine code was retained, but power increased from 80bhp at 4000rpm to a useful 88bhp at 4400rpm.

The 280CE, with the latest headrest design clearly in view through the open side windows.

available for all cars (the centre slide control for the vents was deleted with this set-up, incidentally, airflow being controlled by twisting the eyeball vents, as per the outer pair), height adjustment was fitted to the driver's seat on all grades, and the rear bench seat was modified to make it more comfortable.

On the mechanical front, all cars gained a modified radiator, new brake calipers and pads up front (along with new brake pipes), a two-piece propshaft to replace the original three-piece one, new body shields, modified striker plates for the front door locks, and thinner rear and side windows in a bid to reduce weight. As a bonus for high-mileage users, longer service intervals were introduced on the diesel models and M110-engined cars.

As for specific models, the 250's six-cylinder engine was changed from the 123.920 unit to the 123.921 version. Power went up from 129bhp to 140bhp thanks to new pistons giving an increase in the compression ratio (from 8.7:1 to 9.0:1), revised porting and valve timing, a dual exhaust system, a modified carburettor sitting atop a fresh intake manifold to provide improved top-end performance, and a pre-heater set-up on the carb for faster, cleaner warm-up running. The extra horses justified the use of HR-rated tyres in place of the old SR-rated rubber.

Also in September 1979, the 300D engine was uprated via a modified pre-combustion chamber shape, a new camshaft

Colour & trim summary

A great deal of confusion exists with regard to standard paint colour names, and especially trim and upholstery designations, where the same moniker was often used for a different shade. Depending on the year, ordering material by name only could result in the wrong hue being supplied, and some countries used different names altogether, so this list should help those looking to restore a car to original specification.

September 1979 – September 1981
Standard solid paint colours

No	German name	English name	Other names
040	Schwarz	Black	–
479	Moorbraun	Moor Brown	Walnut Brown
504	Englischrot	English Red	–
673	Saharagelb	Sahara Yellow	–
681	Weizengelb	Wheat Yellow	Manilla Beige
737	Classicweiss	Classic White	–
880	Agavengrün	Agave Green	Cactus Green
934	Chinablau	China Blue	–

Special solid paint colours

No	German name	English name	Other names
476	Goldbraun	Golden Brown	–
482	Apricotorange	Apricot Orange	–
501	Orientrot	Orient Red	–
568	Signalrot	Signal Red	–
618	Mimosengelb	Mimosa Yellow	–
623	Hellelfenbein	Light Ivory	–
680	Heliosgelb	Sun Yellow	–
684	Taigabeige	Taiga Beige	Pastel Beige
740	Pastellgrau	Pastel Grey	–
875	Mangogrün	Mango Green	–

No	German name	English name	Other names
904	Dunkelblau	Dark Blue	Midnight Blue
940	Hansablau	Hansa Blue	Marine Blue

Metallic paint colours

No	German name	English name	Other names
172	Anthrazitgrau	Anthracite Grey	–
473	Champagner	Champagne	–
480	Manganbraun	Manganese Brown	–
581	Inkarot	Inca Red	–
735	Astralsilber	Astral Silver	–
876	Zypressengrün	Cypress Green	–
877	Petrol	Petrol	Blue-Green
881	Silberdistel	Silver Thistle	Thistle Green
930	Silberblau	Silver-Blue	–
932	Lapisblau	Lapis Blue	–

September 1981 – September 1982
Standard solid paint colours

No	German name	English name	Other names
040	Schwarz	Black	–
476	Goldbraun	Golden Brown	–
504	Englischrot	English Red	–
673	Saharagelb	Sahara Yellow	–
681	Weizengelb	Wheat Yellow	Manilla Beige
737	Classicweiss	Classic White	–
880	Agavengrün	Agave Green	Cactus Green
934	Chinablau	China Blue	–

Special solid paint colours

No	German name	English name	Other names
501	Orientrot	Orient Red	–
568	Signalrot	Signal Red	–
623	Hellelfenbein	Light Ivory	–
680	Heliosgelb	Sun Yellow	–
684	Taigabeige	Taiga Beige	Pastel Beige
740	Pastellgrau	Pastel Grey	–
875	Mangogrün	Mango Green	–
904	Dunkelblau	Dark Blue	Midnight Blue
940	Hansablau	Hansa Blue	Marine Blue

Metallic paint colours

No	German name	English name	Other names
172	Anthrazitgrau	Anthracite Grey	–
473	Champagner	Champagne	–
480	Manganbraun	Manganese Brown	–
735	Astralsilber	Astral Silver	–
876	Zypressengrün	Cypress Green	–
877	Petrol	Petrol	Blue-Green
881	Silberdistel	Silver Thistle	Thistle Green
930	Silberblau	Silver-Blue	–
932	Lapisblau	Lapis Blue	–

September 1979 – September 1982
Cloth trim

No	German name	English name	Other names
031	Schwarz	Black	–
032	Blau	Blue	–
034	Dattel	Date	Palomino
035	Creme	Cream	–
036	Olive	Olive	–
037	Siena	Sienna	–

Vinyl trim

No	German name	English name	Other names
131	Schwarz	Black	–
132	Blau	Blue	–
134	Dattel	Date	Palomino
135	Creme	Cream	–
136	Olive	Olive	–
137	Siena	Sienna	–

Leather trim

No	German name	English name	Other names
231	Schwarz	Black	–
232	Blau	Blue	–
234	Dattel	Date	Palomino
235	Creme	Cream	–
236	Olive	Olive	–
237	Siena	Sienna	–

| | | Velour trim | |
No	German name	English name	Other names
931	Schwarz	Black	–
932	Blau	Blue	–
934	Dattel	Date	Palomino
935	Creme	Cream	–
936	Olive	Olive	–
937	Siena	Sienna	–

Prices for the 1980 Model Year cars were released at the end of July 1979 in the domestic market. The 123 series range was huge in Germany, including the 200 saloon at DM 21,041, 230 saloon at DM 22,227, 250 saloon at DM 25,515, 250 long-wheelbase model at DM 38,273, 280 saloon at DM 28,894, 280E saloon at DM 31,075, 200D saloon at DM 22,159, 240D saloon at DM 23,673, 240D lwb model at DM 37,154, 300D saloon at DM 25,809, 300D lwb model at DM 38,567, 230T estate at DM 26,465, 250T estate at DM 29,753, 280TE estate at DM 35,256, 240TD estate at DM 27,911, 300TD estate at DM 30,047, 230C coupé at DM 27,741, 280C coupé at DM 33,007, and 280CE coupé at DM 35,188. As if that wasn't

As if there wasn't already enough choice, the European tuning companies were on hand to modify the 123 series models. AMG, featured here in a Brabus advert (Brabus were still fairly new to the game back then), were perhaps the most famous. Lorinser made some kits for the estates, and some even turned their hand to creating convertibles.

enough to contend with, the engine revisions in September 1979 took the price of the 250 saloon up to DM 26,024, the 250 long-wheelbase car up to DM 38,669, the 250T estate up to DM 30,261, the 300D saloon up to DM 26,148, the 300D lwb model up to DM 38,906, and the 300TD estate up to DM 30,386.

Leading options included alloy wheels (priced at DM 1170), all-weather tyres (DM 164), special paint (DM 237), metallic paint (DM 1023), a manually- or power-operated sunroof (DM 876 and DM 1170, respectively), a passenger-side door mirror (DM 102, but standard on estates), automatic transmission (DM 1831), power steering for base cars (DM 729), cruise control for automatic sixes and the 300D with AT (DM 452), self-levelling suspension (DM 865), an uprated battery (DM 51), air-conditioning (DM 3006, or DM 3593 in fully-automatic guise), auxiliary heating (DM 1655), central locking (DM 350), tinted glass (DM 277 on the saloons, or DM 531 with a laminated windscreen), power windows (DM 661 for the front windows only, or DM 1181 for four), a heated rear screen with laminated safety glass (DM 153), headlight wash/wipe system (DM 480), two-tone horn (DM 203), MB-Tex vinyl trim (DM 198), velour trim (DM 1560), leather trim (DM 1842), seat heaters (for the front seats only now, at DM 497), orthopaedic front seats (DM 95 per side), reinforced front seats (DM 31 per side), luggage nets on the back of the front seats (DM 59), passenger seat height adjustment (DM 95), a folding armrest between the front seats (DM 169), a split rear seat for the estate (DM 548), third row seating for the estate (from DM 944), rear headrests (DM 164 for two), rear compartment lighting (DM 70), rear speakers (DM 277), a glovebox lock (DM 24), a luggage blind for the estates (DM 435), rubber floormats (DM 29), coconut floormats (DM 153), a halon gas fire extinguisher (DM 62), luggage anchors for the estates (DM 51), a heavy load kit for the estates (DM 503), a towbar (DM 531, with the towing weight limit set at 1500kg/3300lb from the start of 1980), the deletion of model type badges on the tail, and the usual choice of stereo equipment.

The supremely elegant W126 S-Class series was introduced at the 1979 Frankfurt Show, powered by 2.8-litre straight-sixes, or all-alloy 3.8- and 5.0-litre V8s. Production began on the state-of-the-art lines at Sindelfingen in December. At the same time Joachim Zahn retired as Chairman of the Board of Management of Daimler-Benz AG, succeeded by Dr Gerhard Prinz.

An M102 cutaway engine that did the rounds at various motor shows.

The fuel-injected M102 E23 engine in situ in a 230E saloon.

The company had a number of interesting vehicles at the Environmental Protection Technology exhibition, including a noise-encapsulated 240D. Cost almost certainly shelved the project, for rising prices were becoming a major headache for the German maker, especially in export markets where the strength of the Deutschmark was pushing them even higher. As it happens, prices increased once more in Germany in March 1980, the cost of 123 series motoring going up by an average of around four per cent – the new streamlined wiper blades, improved screen vent and intermittent rear wiper control for the estates struggling to justify that kind of hike. By now, the 280C was no longer listed anyway, and no replacement was offered either, leaving only the 230C and 280CE pairing in the domestic two-door line-up with the arrival of spring.

The SL/SLC models inherited new, lighter engines in the spring of 1980, with the 123 series gaining the M102 powerplant – a replacement for the M115 lump – not long after, which provided owners with a higher level of performance, greater economy, and longer service intervals. Developed under Hans-Otto Derndinger and presented to the press at the start of June, the four-cylinder M102 was first seen in 102.980 guise, which was a fuel-injected 2.3-litre unit, and transformed the 230 into the 230E, the 230T into the 230TE, etc, at the tail-end of June.

Whilst retaining a cast iron block, angled over to keep height down to a minimum, the M102 was physically smaller than its older counterpart, and lighter thanks to this, a reduction in oil and water capacities, and things like the use of a single-row timing chain rather than a duplex one. This factor alone helped improve fuel economy, but the adoption of a crossflow head with hemispherical combustion chambers added greater efficiency into the equation as well, while the counterweighted crankshaft enhanced refinement.

With mechanically-operated Bosch K-Jetronic fuel-injection, one could be forgiven for thinking this was a scaled-down

One of the first 230TE estates. William Boddy of *Motor Sport* fame said of the 230TE: "On almost every count, the Mercedes-Benz 230 is a very fine product." And if Mr Boddy says that, you can take it as read.

Tail of the 230E saloon, with the new badge being about the only external difference between the old and new cars.

version of the M110 six, but a major difference was the use of a single overhead camshaft on the four-cylinder unit, calling for longer rocker arms to act on the camshaft, which was placed low down in the vee created by the angle of the valve stems. Visual differences compared to the M115s included intake and exhaust positions following M110 practice, breakerless transistorized ignition, a far wider, flatter rocker cover, an oil filter high up at the back of the engine (like the diesels), a dipstick on the same side as the M110 unit (opposite to the M115), and a viscous-coupled cooling fan.

For the 2.3-litre engine, a larger 95.5mm bore and shorter 80.3mm stroke was adopted, giving a capacity of 2299cc. Retaining the 9.0:1 compression ratio of old, the fuel-injected unit gave 136bhp at 5100rpm (a healthy increase of 27bhp), along with 151lbft of torque, cleaner emissions, and around ten per cent better fuel economy.

The automatic transmission on the 230E was basically carried over from the 230, although it did gain a new 722.122

A 230CE coupé that was featured in a lot of the publicity material surrounding the launch of the M102-engined 123 series models.

The 2-litre M102 V20 unit.

Above, left and top: The 200 saloon with M102 power.

designation along the way, as well as a taller 3.58:1 back axle to go with it. The same rear axle ratio was used with the new manual gearbox launched alongside the 230E – the GL68/20B. In the case of the new 2.3-litre car, the type 716.211 version was used, coming with 3.91 on first, 2.32 on second, 1.42 on third, and a direct top. This unit was not only lighter than before, being made in diecast aluminium, it gave smoother shifts, too.

The 2-litre version of the M102 (type 102.920) was put into production in August, at the same time as the press presentation of the forthcoming 200T and 300TDT estate models. In basic summary, the 2-litre engine had a single Stromberg carburettor in place of the fuel-injection system, and lost the trick ignition. Sharing the same stroke measurement as its 2.3-litre counterpart, but having a smaller 89.0mm bore, this combination gave a 1997cc displacement. With 109bhp on tap (an increase of

The 280 saloon from the second half of the 1980 Model Year, with views under the bonnet and in the boot. Note the new carpet trim in the luggage compartment, replacing the old rubber matting as part of the 'Series 2' upgrade.

15bhp), the new 200s were able to adopt a taller 3.69:1 rear axle ratio to go with the manual or automatic gearboxes on offer. The 4MT was the same unit as that used on the 230E, while the optional 4AT was the same W4B025 transmission, but with a unique 722.121 code. With the introduction of the updated 200s, the battery was changed from a 44Ah one to 55Ah,

bringing the entry-level model into line with the other petrol-engined machines.

The first 200 saloons featuring the M102 engine were released at DM 22,555 in Germany, along with the 230E saloon at DM 25,222, the 230CE coupé at DM 30,838, and 230TE at DM 28,781. The 230E special purpose chassis was

Above and overleaf: A late-1980 model 280E saloon, with the interior shots providing the most interest, especially the picture showing the new heater controls that would be adopted officially for the 1981 season. Note also the velour trim (similar in style to the earlier velour upholstery), the manual sunroof, Becker 'Grand Prix' stereo, headlight adjuster, and the old-style seat heater switches.

also available, priced at DM 23,899, which represented a jump of about DM 2000 compared with the old version. Meanwhile, the availability of ABS brakes became more widespread, with all Mercedes passenger cars gaining the option (SA 470) from August 1980 onwards. At the same time, 123 series owners could specify a tachometer (SA 451) on the various petrol-engined grades, along with the turbo-diesels; it took the upper segment of the meter previously occupied solely by the clock. Another change made in readiness for

the 1981 season was the adoption of a new heater with twin slider controls on the console, although this move was made very late in the season.

Things were pretty much the same in America as they had been in the 1979 season, except for the fitment of yellow foglights up front. The 280E and 280CE were the only petrol models in the 123 series line-up, as diesel power continued to dominate the range. This didn't hurt sales, though, as 1980 was another record year, with sales up to almost 54,000 units. The

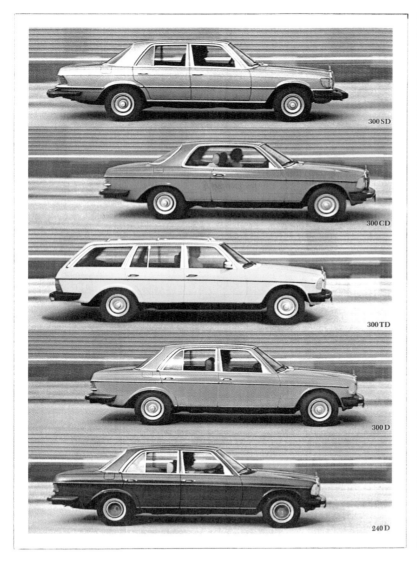

American advertising for the 1980 Model Year range.

$24,569 300TD was the model that captured attention, with *Car & Driver* remarking: "The TD is so wonderfully balanced and so good in all respects, it is not only the best station wagon we've tested, it ranks right up there as one of the all-time best cars in our experience."

In Britain, PAS was now standard on all cars sold through the UK's 97 dealers for 1980, and the petrol-engined estates were sold in automatic guise (this had always been the case with the £11,708 250T, but the manual gearbox option on the £13,837 280TE had been dropped); the pair of 2-litre saloons continued in manual-only trim. Prices were around £800 up on those from the start of the previous season, with the 123 series ranging from £7823 for the manual 200 saloon to £14,640 for the long-wheelbase 240D equipped with an automatic transmission.

After another large price increase for 1979, things settled down a little in Australia for the 1980 season. The 240D provided the entry-level model at $31,642, while the petrol-engined 230 was just over $200 more. Next up the line was the 300D at $34,695, with the 280E topping the saloon range at $38,030, all of which

came with an automatic transmission, although a manual gearbox option was made available on the diesel cars for 1981; the 280CE was still the only coupé, priced at $43,650 for 1980.

Due to exchange rates, most imported cars in Japan were a touch cheaper for the 1979 season, with some makers, such as Volvo, able to pass on large price reductions. The 240D had lost the manual option at this time, meaning all 123 series cars had the 4AT gearbox, and things continued much the same for the 1980 Model Year, except for a subtle price hike. This took the cost of the 240D up to ¥5,100,000, the 230 to ¥5,530,000, the 300D to ¥5,910,000, the 280E to ¥7,030,000, and the 280CE to ¥7,780,000. For comparison, a Rover 3500 was listed at ¥4,650,000, or one could buy around ten lightweight Japanese kei-cars for the same money.

The 1981 model year

The first cars for the 1981 season had their bulkhead and heater box modified to optimize passenger protection in the event of a big accident, and a strut was added to the front suspension to stop the road wheels moving too far in a frontal impact. As well as strengthening in the transmission tunnel, a new front crossmember and radiator mount, the 123 series also gained updated fuel pumps, and the air-conditioning systems from the W126 S-Class, with electrical rather than pneumatic controls. A new heater unit had been adopted by this time, too, with greater control through a pair of sliders above the three rotary switches.

The latest air conditioning control panel.

The new air filter arrangement on the 2.8-litre fuel-injected engine.

Dashboard of a 1981 Model Year estate, distinguished by its rear wash/wipe switches on the console. The key points to note here, though, are the heater controls and the optional tachometer, just visible in the top left-hand corner.

On the mechanical side, a quick start device was added on the diesel engines, and the four-cylinder diesel models got the GL68/20 manual transmission. This was the 20A version (type 716.210) rather than the 20B fitted to the petrol cars, although internal ratios were the same. What was different, however, was the final-drive specifications, with the 200D retaining its 3.92:1 back axle, and the 240D keeping its 3.69:1 one. In addition, the M110 E28 engine used in the 280E-based cars gained a new air filter assembly for the 1981 Model Year.

Domestic prices went up a fraction, with the 200 saloon becoming DM 22,973 in August 1980, while the 300D long-wheelbase model was the most expensive car in the 123 series, commanding DM 41,188. Newcomers included the 200T estate, priced at DM 26,532 and entering production in early November, and the 300TD Turbo-Diesel (or 300TDT) estate, which cost DM 37,143 and started rolling off the line at Bremen a couple of weeks earlier.

Continued page 128

Right and opposite: A couple of 1981 Model Year saloons in quite different settings.

Publicity photograph of the 230CE for the 1981 season.

The 1981 280TE estate.

The new 200T grade, which lowered the price of entry for those looking for a Mercedes station wagon.

A new force to be reckoned with.

The OM617 D30A engine on the testbed, with the exhaust manifold and Garrett turbocharger glowing red.

Left, above and top: The 300TDT model in its natural habitat.

The Mercedes-Benz stand at the 1981 Geneva Show, with S-Class saloons on the left, the SL/SLC at the rear, and the 123 series cars on the right.

There was nothing special about the 200T – it was just a smaller-engined version of the station wagon, possibly due to the increased power available from the 2-litre lump and the 230TE having that much more poke than the 230T it replaced. Even though it was the worst kept secret in the motor industry, the arrival of the luxurious 300TDT (with 280E lights and chrome grilles on the bulkhead) was far more interesting, if only because of the engine – the first turbocharged Mercedes to be fielded in Europe.

A turbo-diesel car had been made available for the press to sample as early as 1976, but it made perfect sense – far more than adding a Garrett T03 turbocharger to a petrol engine. This was basically the same unit as used in the 300SD, with the same leading specifications as the late OM617 D30 unit (2998cc), but with an exhaust-driven turbo adding an 'A' suffix to the engine code and a substantial 33 more horses under the bonnet. Indeed, with a 21.5:1 c/r, the 617.952 five developed a healthy 125bhp at 4350rpm, along with 184lbft of torque – the latter being

enough to eclipse the 2.8-litre petrol engines, but combined with significantly more frugality. In fact, despite its automatic-only status, most contemporary tests found the 300TDT to be more economical than its normally-aspirated sibling.

Incidentally, things got confusing on the stereo front as the 1981 season began, for the 'Mexico' radio/cassette gained an electronic tuner, but strangely took on the SA 510 option code previously used by the 'Monza' unit. It was revised for the 1982 season, and again for 1984 and 1985 (the latter being the most dramatic revision), but then kept going until the demise of the 123 series.

From the spring of 1981, the auxiliary heating system came with a digital rather than analogue display, and there was a revision to the pneumatics on the central locking system at the same time. Other than a modification to the seatbelt roller mechanism in July 1981, the month in which the 280 saloon was dropped from the line-up, there were no other major changes during the season.

On the corporate front, 1981 saw the last of the 600s built, as well as the first of the 126 series coupés – the 380SEC and 500SEC ranking amongst the author's all-time favourites from the postwar era, even though they brought about the end of the SLC series. Airbags and seatbelt pretension systems became listed on certain models during the year, too, keeping Daimler-Benz very much at the forefront of safety innovation and technology.

Looking at the export markets, in America, the big news for the 1981 season revolved around the S-Class machines, but just as importantly, the 300TD station wagon was replaced by the turbocharged 300TDT model. Otherwise, the 240D, 300D and 280E saloons continued alongside the 300CD and 280CE coupés; all cars sold in the US had an automatic gearbox, although the 240D saloon could be specified with a 4MT gearbox if required. Even in manual guise, though, a 0-60 time of 19.7 seconds for the 240D was hardly breathtaking (especially for a car costing the best part of $18,000), and one can see why MBNA were welcoming turbo power with open arms, as were Stateside buyers – diesels accounting for 78 per cent of the 63,000 units sold in 1981.

The $31,000 300TDT was not only significantly quicker than the other diesels on offer, it also had a new emissions system with vacuum-modulated EGR, making it cleaner than

The US-spec 300CD coupé for the 1981 season.

its predecessor, and offered better economy, too, its city/highway gas mileage being rated at 26/30 by the EPA against 24/28 for the outgoing 300TD. For the record, *Road & Track* clocked a 13.2 second 0-60 time with the 300TDT (with a 3.07:1 final-drive), recording speeds of 28mph (45kph), 43mph (69kph), 73mph (117kph) and 102mph (163kph) through the gears.

British buyers were offered the same 123 series line-up as the previous season, although prices increased by around eight per cent – the entry-level 200 saloon was now listed at £8395, while the lwb models hovered around the £15,000 mark. Most people would have been more interested in cars like the 280E saloon at £12,775, or the estsate version at £14,295, however.

Mercedes-Benz (UK) Limited launched the updated 200 and 230E lines during February 1981, with the base car now having a £8700 price-tag, although the 4AT gearbox option was revived on this model for a £615 premium. The 230E saloon was priced at £9501 in manual guise, the 230CE coupé at £11,700, and the 230TE estate at £11,150; the new 200T was listed at £8950, and its 300TD stablemate at £11,600. Leading options included alloy wheels at £454, ABS braking at £830, air-conditioning at £1118, a power sunroof at £435, a manual sunroof at £330, headlamp wash/wipe facility at £178, a tachometer at £73, different trim (with leather at around £700), and a long list of stereo equipment.

Autocar, the UK weekly, tried the 230E saloon and declared: "Overall, the Mercedes is a highly satisfactory car, much more so than the previous smaller-engined saloons in the Daimler-Benz range, and it grows on you greatly the more you drive it."

Rival *Motor* went for the 230CE with an automatic gearbox. Having recorded a 0-60 time of 10.3 seconds and a 21.3mpg average fuel consumption figure, it concluded: "The new fuel-injected four gives Mercedes' popular small coupé much

better performance (though still nothing special for the price) and improved economy allied to very impressive mechanical refinement. The smooth four-speed automatic and taut handling are also plus points, though rear accommodation is cramped by class standards. Build and finish are, as always, superb."

As it happens, *Autocar* also mentioned the legendary Stuttgart build quality in a 230TE test from later in the year, noting: "No-one can fail to admire the wonderful attention to detail and the precision fit and finish in the 230TE, which are sure to be a lasting delight for the owner."

The 1981 Model Year was quite significant for Australian buyers, as two estate models joined the existing W123 line-up of four saloons (two with diesel lumps and two with petrol engines) and a single fuel-injected coupé. Using the AT versions as a yardstick, the 230 saloon was priced at $31,870, the 240D at $32,209, the 300D at $35,305, and the 280E at $38,703. The 230E was released in July 1981 as an early 1982 model, by the way, replacing the 230 saloon and coming with a $32,440 sticker price in its most basic form. As for the coupé, the 280CE was listed at $44,419 at this time, while the two estates – the 300TD

A W123 taxi alongside the Auto 2000 concept car, first displayed at the 1981 Frankfurt Show.

and 280TE – came in at $39,355 and $42,340, respectively. A price increase was applied to the station wagons in January 1981, incidentally, adding about $700 to the base price, while an automatic transmission for the diesel variant added a further $2060 to the invoice.

In Japan, the 123 series range consisted of the 230, 280E, 240D, 300D, 280CE and 300TD models, with prices starting at ¥6,020,000. All cars came with automatic transmission only, and were duly carried over for the start of the 1982 season. And that's what we look at next …

The 1982 model year

The easiest change to spot for the 1982 season was the fresh paint palette, with a number of coachwork colours dropped in September, and others changing status. However, the door locks and glovebox were modified at the same time, and an overrun cut-off valve was added on cars with fuel-injection to save petrol.

The 230E's ignition system was improved and the engine tweaked to give a lower idle speed, and manual 250 models were given a taller 3.58:1 rear axle ratio in order to enhance fuel consumption. Ironically, a lot of the benefit was probably lost through higher rolling resistance, though, as the 250 saloon adopted the 195/70 rubber that was already standard on the 250T estate.

The automatic transmission on the 250- and 280E-based models was also changed, with the W4B025 unit giving way to the W4B040 design from the S-Class, which featured smoother downshifts, easier access to kickdown scenarios, and programming that encouraged faster upshifts and second gear starts in a bid to save fuel. The 250s employed the 722.308 version of the new gearbox, while the 280Es used the 722.309 model, although both shared the same 3.68, 2.41, 1.44 and 1.00 cogs, and both lines retained the old back axle ratios.

For the record, the German 123 series line-up looked like this in September 1981. There was the 200 saloon at DM 23,764, the 230E saloon at DM 26,724, the 250 saloon at DM 28,532, the 250 lwb model at DM 42,398, the 280E saloon at DM 34,194, the 200D saloon at DM 24,272, the 240D saloon at DM 25,933, the 240D lwb model at DM 40,703, the 300D saloon at DM 28,645, the 300D lwb model at DM 42,624, the 200T estate at DM 27,448, the 230TE estate at DM 30,408, the 250T estate

A 1982 Model Year 240TD coming to the rescue.

One of the last 280TEs to feature chrome grilles on the bulkhead.

131

at DM 32,216, the 280TE estate at DM 37,810, the 240TD estate at DM 29,617, the 300TD estate at DM 32,330, the 300TDT estate at DM 38,420, the 230CE coupé at DM 32,634, and the 280CE coupé at DM 38,714.

From October, the GL275 five-speed manual gearbox became available as an option (SA 428), with the diesel-engined and 250- and 280E-based cars adopting the GL275A (type 717.400) unit, and the 200- and 230E-based ones the GL275B (717.401). Both came with internal ratios of 3.82 on first, 2.20 on second, 1.40 on third, 1.00 on fourth, and an overdriven 0.81 fifth; final-drives were carried over from the 4MT specifications. First through fourth was in a traditional 'H' pattern, with fifth up to the right, and reverse below that.

During November, the central locking system was modified on the coupés, and plastic liners were added to the inner front wheelarches on all cars. There was also a new, rarely-taken option of a modified front armrest on the door with a lidded storage box and lock (SA 920 or SA 921 depending on the side).

Cars about to be shipped to America, with the new 'Turbo-Diesel' badge on the tail of the saloon nearest the camera. The saloon on the upper deck has a 'Diesel' one, allowing us to tie this down as the start of the 1982 season, when vehicles already on the line would have mingled with the latest variants.

Above and top: The optional airbag installation.

An airbag and integrated seatbelt-tensioner arrangement was available as an option for all models from January 1982 (SA 442), and the locking mechanism on the bonnet was modified to help prevent theft. As it happens, this was becoming a major concern for urbanites, and an alarm system (SA 551) was offered during the summer.

In the meantime, domestic prices increased in January 1982, going up by around three per cent, before another price hike in the summer, of again around three per cent. This took the cheapest 200 saloon to DM 24,996, while the 280CE coupé commanded a hefty DM 40,962 (the flagship of the 123 series line if we ignore the specialist long-wheelbase cars). The 250T estate disappeared in August 1982.

The 300DT saloon for the US market.

The turbocharged 300CDT coupé, or 300CD as it was known in the showrooms. The 'T' suffix, as added to the 300DT caption on the same page, simply helps with identification.

133

In America, MBNA's love of diesel soared to new heights, as the petrol-engined 123 series cars were dropped at the end of the 1981 season, leaving only a handful of S-Class models and an expanded range of 123 series diesels in the US showrooms. Both the 300D saloon and 300CD coupé gained turbocharged-engines to create the 300DT (type 123.133) and 300CDT (123.153) – unique to the North American and Japanese markets, they were augmented by a 240D saloon (now with EGR) and a 300TDT estate in the US for 1982. Despite high prices, with the 105mph (168kph) 300CD being over $32,000, for instance, sales continued to boom for the 407 dealers Stateside, with yet another sales record set after almost 66,000 cars were moved in 1982. Incidentally, automatic air-conditioning and full wood consoles had become a standard feature on the US-spec cars by this time.

In Britain, the range and prices were carried over from February 1981, while in Australia, for 1982, the 240D saloon was the cheapest W123 model, starting at $32,209. Next up was the 230E at $35,238 (about half the price of the contemporary 380SEL), while the 300D was listed at $36,883, and the 280E at $43,027. As for the estates, the 280TE was $47,586, and the 300TD $41,999 in manual guise, or $44,037 with an automatic transmission. The sporting 280CE coupé was also carried over, priced at $46,926 for the 1982 season.

Alternative power

After the second fuel crisis started to bite, in 1979, the industrialized nations had begun to realize that their reliance on oil was a major potential long-term issue, and people started to look seriously at alternative options. Air quality was also a

An early W123 saloon converted to run on methanol fuel.

One of the W123 saloons that took part in the 'Alternative Drives' programme, initiated in 1979 on vans, with passenger cars joining the fray in 1980.

The bi-fuel 200 with its huge LPG tank dominating the boot.

concern – smog in areas like California and the major cities in Japan was at last starting to clear as a result of tentative regulation to reduce harmful emissions.

Daimler-Benz had begun research into alternative fuels and motive power much earlier. Methanol SLs were created to build data on running characteristics as early as 1974, followed by methanol- and electric-powered vans, a methanol W123 saloon, and a 280E built with a petrol-hydrogen bi-fuel arrangement during 1977. There was also a large-scale 1979 'Alternative Drives' test programme using methanol and ethanol fuels, with no fewer than 80 vehicles involved.

However, as the energy question became pressing, a higher profile was given to this valuable research. The 1981 Frankfurt Show witnessed the debut of a 200 saloon converted to operate on both petrol and liquefied petroleum gas (LPG). From the middle of 1982, this factory-made bi-fuel machine was offered to a number of markets. It was easy to identify, as the huge LPG tank in the boot was fed by a second filler located underneath the original one. However, the conversion was never really popular: the initial cost of the 200 was high before the LPG installation (which cost around DM 3000), and normal users would simply never get to recoup their investment in fuel savings.

Not long after the LPG car took its first bow, in April 1982, Daimler-Benz displayed an electric-powered estate at the Hannover Trade Fair at Hannover Messe. This was fitted with a 30kW electric motor and a huge bank of nickel-iron batteries weighing around 600kg (1320lb)! Although real-world testing in the estate, and a number of vans before it, revealed that the project had potential, the impracticality of regular charging and outrageous cost of battery replacement a couple of years down the line quickly shelved the proposal.

Shown alongside the electric car was a bi-fuel 280TE with hydrogen power backing up the petrol supply. Hydrogen has long been the darling of 'Green' engineers, but at that time, suitable storage systems that allowed a decent range were simply not available. Even if they had been, the infrastructure wasn't really in place to keep the idea alive. This one was ahead of its time, although Germany's Federal Ministry for Research & Technology supported a 1984 test programme that involved no fewer than five 280TE estates and five 310 vans.

Above and right: The electric-powered estate of 1982 vintage. This huge bank of batteries was the only viable option at the time, with the idea of a sliding tray having been employed at Daimler-Benz over a decade earlier.

The petrol-hydrogen bi-fuel 280TE, with views of the engine, hydrogen storage arrangement, and a car on test in 1984.

6
Competition history

The W123 series hardly has a strong image when one thinks back to the glorious motorsport scene that existed in the seventies and early eighties. Grids were varied at race circuits, but it has to be said, it's hard to remember a Benz saloon. Rallying was still a sport where the privateer could walk away with the silverware, although few tried their hand with such a heavy beast. Dig deep enough, though, and one will find that the W123 models had a quite distinguished competition history …

As far as the W123 series was concerned, there was no real race history to speak of when the cars were new. Ultimately, the various models were either too heavy or lacking in horses (or both!) for track work, although Bert Baustian of Germany did have a 280CE prepared for racing. Sponsored by Leba Hartpapier & Hargewebe GmbH, it was booked for a couple of major races at the Nürburgring in 1982 (including the ADAC 1000km Race), but failed to turn up on both occasions. However, various models from the line can be seen in today's historic racing events, staged all over the world.

The story doesn't end there, though – far from it, actually, as the rugged chassis and reliable drivetrain made the W123 eminently suitable for the contemporary rally scene, especially the long-distance events where outright speed was less important than it was in the majority of World Rally Championship (WRC) rounds.

Erich Waxenberger, who had earlier made his name via the marque's touring cars, was named head of the latest Mercedes-Benz rally team, and the 280E was duly homologated as a Group 2 car (homologation number 5633) in July 1976. The Group 2 classification left little room for serious modification (nothing more than blueprinting, a minute overbore, a new exhaust, lubrication system, different gearing and the uprating of similar components was allowed), but at least it was easier

The 280E was homologated as a Group 2 machine in July 1976.

to make a competitive machine of the W123 in this arena – the more ambitious Group 4 Class, which was the main one for the majority of the top WRC teams, would be left to the big 450SLCs.

Eventually, it was decided to leave the bore and stroke the same as the showroom models, but increase the compression ratio to 9.0:1. This took the engine power up to 200bhp at 6000rpm, and maximum torque up to 184lbft at 5000rpm. Combined with a four-speed manual transmission and a lighter overall weight (the FIA papers suggested 3069lb/1395kg) thanks to the usual deletion of unwanted parts, it became a viable project. Having said that, of course, it was still a real heavyweight, but it could at least compete with the likes of the Peugeot 504 Coupé in the power-to-weight stakes, and that was always going to provide the biggest threat to the Mercedes in the type of events Waxenberger had in mind.

Interior of the remarkably civilized works rally car. Note the Halda trip, basic heating system, and modified switchgear.

The London-Sydney Rally

The 1977 London-Sydney Rally, otherwise known as the Singapore Airlines Rally, provided an ideal stage to give the 280E its competition debut. This was the fourth, last and longest of the marathons held during the sixties and seventies. The first had been the 1968 London-Sydney Marathon, which was won by Andrew Cowan, Brian Coyle and Colin Malkin driving a Hillman Hunter. The second was the 1970 London-Mexico World Cup Rally, while the third was the little-known forerunner to the Paris-Dakar Rally – the 1974 London-Sahara-Munich World Cup Rally.

The 1977 event was supposed to be over 30 days, but ended up a lot longer due to logistical problems, although the 18,750 miles (30,000km) route format was more or less retained. Starting in London on 14 August, the cars crossed Europe, heading down to Greece before turning towards India; island-hopping through Malaysia and Singapore allowed them to start a huge trek across Australia before reaching the finish in Sydney.

Waxenberger was a wily character, and knew speed merchants were not the ideal choice for an event like this. He was also very aware of the public gaze on the 1977 marathon,

Andrew Cowan photographed with the 280E he used on the 1977 London-Sydney Rally. The Rank Organisation was responsible for all manner of film- and radio-based entertainment at the time, including the iconic *Carry On* movies.

and for that reason, the cars from Germany were officially listed as private entries, just in case disaster struck, with sponsorship covering the two UK-based equipes.

Of 69 crews that made the start, no fewer than seven Mercedes 280Es set off from London. Herbert Kleint, Günther Klapproth and Herbert Vormbruck shared car number 27; Andrew Cowan, Colin Malkin and Mike Broad were in car 33, sponsored by movie moguls The Rank Organisation; Joachim Warmbold, Hans Willemsen and Jean Todt were in number 37; Tony Fowkes and Peter O'Gorman were in the Johnsons Rally Wax-sponsored car 49; Malaysians Swee Chew Wong and Seng Choy Wong were in number 51; Alfred Kling, Klaus Kaiser and Jörg Leininger shared car 59, and Wolfgang Mauch and Jose Dolhem were in car 80.

Amazingly, given the distance involved and the rough terrain, 47 teams made it to the finish. The Mercedes-Benz runners in cars 37, 51 and 80 had fallen by the wayside en route, but overall, the event was a resounding success for the Stuttgart

The 280E shared by Herbert Kleint, Günther Klapproth and Herbert Vormbruck for the London-Sydney Rally. They finished the event in eighth overall.

Joachim Warmbold, Hans Willemsen and Jean Todt (later Ferrari's F1 team boss) kicking up dust in car number 37. Unfortunately, this was one of the three 280Es that failed to make it to Sydney.

A service halt in a friendly garage during the London-Sydney Rally.

The Fowkes/O'Gorman car (registration SPG 679R) pictured in south-eastern Europe en route to second place in the 1977 London-Sydney Rally. Johnson would also sponsor Mercedes' UK-based rally effort with the 450SLC.

maker: Cowan and his men claimed what seemed like an easy victory, with Fowkes and O'Gorman second, just ahead of Paddy Hopkirk's Citroën CX2400. Then came another Citroën and a Peugeot, with Kling's 280E in sixth; Kleint's Benz was eighth, narrowly beaten by another Citroën.

Andrew Cowan (later Mitsubishi's rally team boss) noted of his Mercedes-Benz experience: "I was very impressed by their attitude, and how quickly they had learnt. Most of our testing has

Cowan and his crew sensing that the finish is near…

Above and right: A picture of the car shared by Alfred Kling, Klaus Kaiser and Jörg Leininger, which duly finished the London-Sydney Rally in sixth place, and an advert from Mobil Oil issued just after the event showing the same image, but retouched to resemble the winning Cowan machine. I love this sort of thing!

been done during recces, although some additional testing was done at Bagshot. The car is comfortable and very enjoyable. It is a big, heavy motor car, but for the type of events we are doing, I would say that was their only disadvantage."

The 1978 Safari Rally

The Safari Rally (held 23-27 March, and staged over 3135 miles/5016km of rough road) was the only WRC qualifier tackled by the works with the W123 models in 1978. The four Group 2 280Es were officially entered by Mercedes' African

The 280E of Tony Fowkes and Klaus Kaiser on the 1978 Safari Rally.

importer, DT Dobie, although everyone knew that Stuttgart was behind the team.

Waxenberger put together an incredibly experienced team of drivers and co-drivers. Unfortunately, the local pairing of Joginder Singh and David Doig (past Safari winners in car number 2) went out very early after water entered the engine crossing a swollen river, and the same fate befell the Andrew Cowan/Johnstone Syer machine (number 9) 13 stages later; Sobieslaw Zasada and co-driver Blazej Krupa were clever, and had the air intake raised through a freshly-cut hole in the bonnet

in car number 18. Just over a third of the way through the event, the Tony Fowkes/Klaus Kaiser 280E (number 12) holed its sump after hitting a submerged rock in yet another water hazard, but at least Zasada got to the end in Nairobi, finishing sixth overall and second in Class, albeit a long way off the pace of the winning Peugeot, and the two Porsches and a Datsun that filled the next three places. It has to be said, though, Mercedes was unlucky having to face such wet weather, which caused ten of the 75 time controls to be cancelled. Just to finish was an achievement that particular year – of the 72 starters, only 13 got to the end.

Sobieslaw Zasada, who finished the 1978 Safari Rally in sixth place.

SÜDAMERIKA-RALLYE (17. Aug. - 24. Sept. 1978)
Start und Ziel Buenos Aires (Argentinien)
ca. 30.000 Kilometer durch 10 Staaten mit
Serien-Fahrzeugen

A route plan of the 1978 Rally of South America.

1978 Vuelta a la America del Sud

Given the disastrous results in Kenya, no-one could have foreseen the assault launched on the gruelling 17,875 mile (28,600km) Rally of South America later in the year. Although a non-WRC event, the five-week long rally, held from 17 August to 24 September, certainly managed to attract a high-class field and the attention of the media.

Of the 57 cars competing, no fewer than four 450SLCs and four 280Es were entered by the works for this epic marathon, taking in almost the entire south American continent (Argentina, Uraguay, Paraguay, Brazil, Venezuela, Colombia, Ecuador, Peru, Bolivia and Chile) along the way.

Only 22 crews made it to the prize-giving, with Andrew Cowan and Colin Malkin duly winning the event in car number 421 (a surprisingly standard-looking 450SLC, inside and out), while two of the other SLCs finished second thanks to Sobieslaw Zazada and Andrzej Zembrzuski, and fourth, courtesy of Timo Makinen and Jean Todt. While the fourth SLC failed to finish due

144

to transmission trouble, all of the 280Es got to the end: Tony Fowkes and Klaus Kaiser were a creditable third in car number 422; Herbert Kleint and Günther Klapproth were fifth in number 408; Alfred Kling and Albert Pfuhl were ninth (car 411) behind a Toyota and a couple of Renaults, and Elpidio Caballero and Jurgen Nathan were tenth in car number 407. Granted, these last-named teams were a long way off the pace, around 12 hours behind the winners, but the Fowkes machine was within 33 minutes of Cowan, which is a remarkable achievement.

Swan song

The W123 series cars were never really involved in the European Rally Championship (ERC). They certainly didn't figure in the results, let's put it that way! In addition, the 450SLC would be the weapon of choice for a more serious assault on the World Rally Championship, its campaign starting in earnest during the 1979 season.

As such, appearances of the W123 models were very limited following the Rally of South America. On saying that, three Group 2 280Es were lined up alongside three Group 4 450SLC for the 1979 Safari (ran from 12 April to 16 April). There were 66 starters and 21 finishers, with the Andrew Cowan/Johnstone Syer car (number 16) coming a gallant fourth, second in Class, despite a PAS failure; the big V8s took second and sixth overall. The Zasada 280E (number 19) was

Andrew Cowan, winner of the South American epic in a 450SLC, and a great ambassador for the W123 models.

The 280E of Cowan/Syer on the 1979 Safari Rally. It finished the event in fourth overall.

145

Andrew Cowan pushing his 280CE hard during the 1980 Rally Codasur, held in Argentina in July. This particular coupé was registered S-DY 6804.

taken out in an accident just beyond the halfway mark, while the Singh machine limped home in 11th after damaged engine mountings slowed its charge.

Later in the year, Kyosti Hamalainen entered a 300D in the 1000 Lakes Rally, and won the diesel category after finishing in 31st. It was a crafty way to take a Class victory, but a win is a win, and no-one blinks an eyelid at the thought of diesel racing cars nowadays!

In 1980, when the SLCs came good, there was a single Group 2 280CE for Ingvar Carlsson and Claes Billstam to use in the Acropolis Rally in May, although it was lost in a fire close to the end. The works had another go in the Rally Codasur two months later, with Andrew Cowan and Klaus

Kaiser lying fifth at one stage, before a broken head gasket put them out of the event. Ingvar Carlsson was called up again for the Motogard Rally in New Zealand, but crashed the 280CE at the start of the third day whilst lying seventh. This was to be the last official sortie for the W123, although an odd 280CE was spotted in German ERC events during the year, with Holger Bohne and Adolf Ahrens actually winning the 1980 Saarland Rally in April, fending off the challenge of a pair of Ford Escort RSs.

On 17 December 1980, only three days after its win on the Ivory Coast Rally, Mercedes-Benz announced its withdrawal from the World Rally Championship. Another motorsport era in Stuttgart had come to an end all too quickly …

7

Face-lift and finale

The success of the 123 series models had exceeded all expectations, but it was now in its twilight years. The launch of the smaller W201 and forthcoming W124 were given priority, as these represented the future of the Stuttgart company. The 123s did, however, go out with a bang, gaining some minor styling enhancements and more creature comforts ...

The 1983 Model Year cars (announced in September 1982) were given a wide-ranging, albeit largely cosmetic face-lift. Known as 'Series 3' models, they featured the rectangular headlights previously reserved for the more expensive grades, black bulkhead grilles for all cars in all countries, wider dirt deflector trim on the A-post and C-pillar in chrome and black to reduce wind noise, new paint and trim colours, new seals on the front doors, the option of power-adjusted passenger-side mirror (standard on estates), reshaped backrests on the rear bench seat (with a stronger curve) and new backs on the front seats to allow greater legroom in the rear compartment, Zebrano wood on the fascia (as well as the entire centre console on the coupés, and the upright section on the top saloons and estates, aping the situation already found on 1981 cars in the US), fresh inner door trim panels with fabric inserts, cloth on side trim sections instead of MB-Tex vinyl, velour carpets on 280E/TE/CE and 300TDT models, upgraded material on the rear parcel shelf, modern all-black rocker switches for the power window and seat heater options, plastic window winders and rear roof-mounted grab handles from the soon-to-be-released W201 saloon, a delay function on the interior light and a contact switch added to the rear doors, modified lighting on the HVAC controls, the footrest and rear speaker covers colour-keyed to the interior rather than black (even though it took catalogues a while to catch up on this fact), revised (optional) rear headrests

One of the first 'Series 3' models built was the two-millionth 123 series car produced at the Sindelfingen plant – a 200D saloon.

that were angled over to improve rearward vision, the option of a sunvisor with an illuminated mirror (SA 543), and an economy display added to the lower section of the left-hand combination gauge for petrol-engined cars. On the mechanical front, power-assisted steering was now standard on all cars, as was breakerless ignition on all petrol engines.

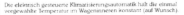

Die elektrisch gesteuerte Klimatisierungsautomatik hält die einmal vorgewählte Temperatur im Wageninneren konstant (auf Wunsch).

Die Mittelkonsole in Zebrano-Holz mit umschäumtem Automatik-Wahlhebel und den Bedienungselementen

The coupés also gained new wood trim, and more of it, as before. These catalogue images show the new switches for the windows and seat heaters perfectly, with matching hazard warning light switch, the speaker fader, and the toggle for the optional passenger-side mirror. On the upper section, we can see a Becker 'Mexico' radio/cassette (a far cry from the 1976 units!), air conditioning controls, the headlight adjuster, and switches for the rear lighting, power sunroof and heated rear window.

The latest 'Series 3' interior upgrade, seen here on a base saloon with a manual transmission, with the new cloth upholstery, door trim, wood garnish on the dashboard, and revised minor switchgear. The cloth was this pattern on all cars, while the velour trim was similar to the earlier version again, and heavier perforations were brought back for the vinyl and leather options.

The mainstream 'Series 3' line-up on the road …

The 1983 season

The domestic 123 series line-up was as extensive as ever, including the 200 saloon at DM 25,815, 230E saloon at DM 28,945, 250 saloon at DM 30,341, 250 lwb model at DM 45,064, 280E saloon at DM 36,375, 200D saloon at DM 26,369, 240D saloon at DM 28,109, 240D lwb model at DM 42,940, 300D saloon at DM 30,465, 300D lwb model at DM 45,302, 200T estate at DM 29,781, 230TE estate at DM 32,911, 280TE estate at DM 40,296, 240TD estate at DM 32,075, 300TD estate at DM 34,431, 300TDT estate at DM 40,940, 230CE coupé at DM 34,521, and 280CE coupé at DM 40,962.

Options included alloy wheels (priced at DM 1362), all-weather tyres (DM 192), special paint (DM 282), metallic paint (DM 1124), a manually- or power-operated sunroof (DM 1017 and DM 1356, respectively), headlight wash/wipe system (DM 537), an electrically-adjusted passenger-side door mirror (DM 192, but standard on estates), alarm (DM 751), a five-speed manual gearbox (DM 1040), automatic transmission (DM 2107), cruise control (DM 525), a tachometer (DM 226), ABS brakes (DM 2712), self-levelling suspension (DM 1006), an SRS airbag (DM 1763), uprated battery (DM 60), air-conditioning (DM 3480, or DM 4181 in fully-automatic guise), auxiliary heating (DM 1932), auxiliary heating for the rear of the estate (DM 932), central locking (DM 412), tinted glass (DM 333 on the saloons, or DM 621 with a laminated windscreen), power windows (DM 774 for the front windows only, or DM 1373 for four), a heated rear screen with laminated safety glass (DM 180), two-tone 'Alpine' horn (DM 243), MB-Tex vinyl trim (DM 232), velour trim (DM 1808), leather trim (DM 2181), front seat heaters (DM 622), orthopaedic front seats (DM 111 per side), reinforced front seats (DM 36 per side), luggage nets

This saloon was featured in the first 'Series 3' catalogue, although the author has no idea what grade it is. The beauty of the face-lift, at least from an owners' point of view, was the standardized look across the range.

An early face-lifted coupé, identified by the black grilles on the bulkhead. This particular car has French-specification lighting.

A 1983 Model Year saloon with the optional headlight wash/wipe system and passenger-side mirror.

A couple of views of the 'Series 3' estate at the time of its launch.

on the back of the front seats (DM 70), passenger seat height adjustment (DM 111), a folding armrest between the front seats (DM 203), a split rear seat for the estate (DM 633), third row seating for the estate (from DM 1073 to DM 1379, depending on the trim), rear headrests (DM 192 for two, or DM 288 for the three used in estate models), rear compartment lighting (DM 85), rear speakers (DM 332), an aerial (from DM 102 for a manual one up to DM 475 for an automatic version supplied without a radio), radio suppression kit and fitting (DM 85, but made FOC soon after), a sunvisor with illuminated mirror (DM 107), glovebox lock (DM 29), a luggage blind for the estates (DM 497), rubber floormats (DM 38), coconut floormats (DM 165), a fire extinguisher (DM 141), luggage anchors for the estates (DM 57), a heavy load kit for the estates (DM 588), a towbar (DM 621), the deletion of model type badges on the tail, and the usual choice of stereo equipment.

There were more changes to the Becker stereo line-up during the summer of 1982, when the SA 515 'Avus' radio with traffic news (identified by the 'Kurier' moniker) made its debut. Costing around DM 605, it was given rubber control knobs for 1984. In the meantime, in February 1983, the 'Grand Prix' radio with electronic tuner (SA 513) was added to the option list, with a 'Grand Prix' radio/cassette version following a couple of weeks later, taking on the SA 511 code once used by the old 'Mexico' range in the process. (Recycling codes was a necessity given the limited range of three-digit numbers.) Both continued until the end of W123 production, the one costing around DM 1150, and the other, with cassette, about DM 300 more. The 'Avus' radio/ cassette (SA 518) had been added in March 1983, too, which duly gained a digital tracking feature as the W123 run came to an end.

At the time of the 'Series 3' launch, regular radio prices ranged from around DM 678 to DM 2124. But before moving

Colour & trim summary

A great deal of confusion exists with regard to standard paint colour names, and especially trim and upholstery designations, where the same moniker was often used for a different shade. Depending on the year, ordering material by name only could result in the wrong hue being supplied, and some countries used different names altogether, so this list should help those looking to restore a car to original specification.

September 1982 – September 1984
Standard solid paint colours

No	German name	English name	Other names
427	Braun	Brown	Russet Brown
585	Altrot	Old Red	Mesa Red
673	Saharagelb	Sahara Yellow	–
681	Weizengelb	Wheat Yellow	Manilla Beige
737	Classicweiss	Classic White	–
751	Liasgrau	Lias Grey	Ascot Grey
803	Riedgrün	Reed Green	Moss Green
900	Surfblau	Surf Blue	Deep Blue

Special solid paint colours

No	German name	English name	Other names
040	Schwarz	Black	–
312	Labradorblau	Labrador Blue	Biscayne Blue
444	Sandbeige	Sand Beige	–
501	Orientrot	Orient Red	–
568	Signalrot	Signal Red	–
623	Hellelfenbein	Light Ivory	–
684	Taigabeige	Taiga Beige	Pastel Beige
822	Eibengrün	Yew Green	Forest Green
904	Dunkelblau	Dark Blue	Midnight Blue

Metallic paint colours

No	German name	English name	Other names
172	Anthrazitgrau	Anthracite Grey	–
473	Champagner	Champagne	–
480	Manganbraun	Manganese Brown	–
735	Astralsilber	Astral Silver	–
876	Zypressengrün	Cypress Green	–
877	Petrol	Petrol	Blue-Green
881	Silberdistel	Silver Thistle	Thistle Green

| 930 | Silberblau | Silver-Blue | – |
| 932 | Lapisblau | Lapis Blue | – |

September 1984 onwards
Standard solid paint colours

No	German name	English name	Other names
459	Maroonbraun	Maroon-Brown	Mocca
540	Barolorot	Barolo Red	Desert Red
681	Weizengelb	Wheat Yellow	Manilla Beige
737	Classicweiss	Classic White	–
751	Liasgrau	Lias Grey	Ascot Grey
803	Riedgrün	Reed Green	Moss Green
900	Surfblau	Surf Blue	Deep Blue

Special solid paint colours

No	German name	English name	Other names
040	Schwarz	Black	–
444	Sandbeige	Sand Beige	–
568	Signalrot	Signal Red	–
623	Hellelfenbein	Light Ivory	–
684	Taigabeige	Taiga Beige	Pastel Beige
822	Eibengrün	Yew Green	Forest Green
904	Dunkelblau	Dark Blue	Midnight Blue

Metallic paint colours

No	German name	English name	Other names
172	Anthrazitgrau	Anthracite Grey	–
199	Blauschwarz	Blue-Black	Black Pearl
355	Diamantblau	Diamond Blue	–
473	Champagner	Champagne	–
480	Manganbraun	Manganese Brown	–
587	Pajettrot	Pajett Red	Cabernet Red

No	German name	English name	Other names
702	Rauchsilber	Smoke Silver	–
735	Astralsilber	Astral Silver	–
876	Zypressengrün	Cypress Green	–
877	Petrol	Petrol	Blue-Green
881	Silberdistel	Silver Thistle	Thistle Green
929	Nautikblau	Nautical Blue	–

September 1982 onwards
Cloth trim

No	German name	English name	Other names
051	Schwarz	Black	–
052	Blau	Blue	–
054	Dattel	Date	Palomino
055	Creme	Cream	Beige
056	Dunkelolive	Dark Olive	Dark Green
057	Hennarot	Henna Red	–

Vinyl trim

No	German name	English name	Other names
151	Schwarz	Black	–
152	Blau	Blue	–
154	Dattel	Date	Palomino
155	Creme	Cream	Beige
156	Dunkelolive	Dark Olive	Dark Green
157	Hennarot	Henna Red	–

Leather trim

No	German name	English name	Other names
251	Schwarz	Black	–
252	Blau	Blue	–
254	Dattel	Date	Palomino
255	Creme	Cream	Beige
256	Dunkelolive	Dark Olive	Dark Green
257	Hennarot	Henna Red	–

Velour trim

No	German name	English name	Other names
951	Anthrazit	Anthracite	Black
952	Blau	Blue	–
954	Dattel	Date	Palomino
955	Creme	Cream	Beige
956	Dunkelolive	Dark Olive	Dark Green
957	Hennarot	Henna Red	–

on, mention should be made of the mobile phone installations, which were available, but cost in the region of DM 20,000 – yes, that is four zeros, and now go back and check on the car prices! Becker and TeKaDe versions were listed, but the chances of coming across one are very remote indeed given the truly astronomical price-tag.

The optional rubber floormats were duly revised in February 1983, going a little more upmarket, while April saw the start of a gradual shift from the W4B025 automatic gearbox to the new W4A020 unit on the less-powerful 123 series machines. Coming with internal ratios of 4.25 on first, 2.41 on second, 1.49 on third and a direct top (final-drive ratios were carried over, incidentally), the 230E-based models gained it first (type 722.401), closely followed by the 200s (722.406), and the diesel-engined cars at the start of summer – the 200D adopting the 722.407 version, the 240D variants the 722.404, and 300Ds the 722.405 model.

While these changes were taking place, an automatic cut-out timer was added to the heated seats option.

Meanwhile, an all-new compact car, the 190/190E (type W201), was announced in November 1982, bringing forth a predecessor to today's C-Class. A diesel-powered 190D was added in 1983, along with a high-performance 16v model, which managed to claim a number of world speed records a few weeks before it was launched on the marketplace. The 2.3-litre petrol W201 was a particularly important addition to the American market, for its superior fuel economy allowed MBNA to curb its reliance on diesel-powered cars to meet the dreaded CAFE mandate. It could even offset the average enough to bring back some of the bigger, more profitable S-Class machines.

On the subject of America, the US-bound cars continued to sport their unique bumpers and headlight units, the latter

With the launch of the W201 (foreground), the Mercedes range was quite extensive. Next to the newcomer, we have the C123, W123 and S123, and in the back row, the R107 SL, and the three S-Class variants – the SEC, SE and SEL. We shouldn't forget the availability of the G-Wagen, too.

The 190E (left) and 240D on display at the 1983 Geneva Show.

continuing with yellow foglights until the end of 123 series production. MBNA listed eight cars, ranging from the $22,470 240D sedan up to the $53,570 380SEC coupé. The 123 series models included the aforementioned 240D saloon, the 300DT turbo-diesel saloon, the 300CDT coupé, and the $33,850 300TDT estate, all carried over from the previous season. The latter was a pricey tool, but as *Motor Trend* said at the time: "If you can bite the $30K bullet, the projected low operating costs and high resale value almost make the 300TDT an economy car."

And in a separate test that brought together four contemporary station wagons, the same magazine found that "away from the test track, the 300TDT's powertrain, as well as its sophisticated chassis, continued to impress. Even staff members who are not particularly sympathetic toward diesel power, and who think most German machinery is overpriced, found themselves trying to spirit away the TD for long weekend cruises. Engineering is the car's real message, and it shows up best on choppy, rippled pavement. The road noise rises, but the chassis soaks up wheel motion and remains composed and stable. Combinations of speed, cornering load and surface roughness that would have other cars lurching and slewing about were accommodated by the Mercedes without drama. That's where all that money goes." 1983 was another record year for US sales, by the way, with almost 74,000 cars finding new owners.

The UK distributors carried much the same extensive range as before, with all 123 series models having the option of a manual or automatic gearbox, the latter adding £643 to the invoice on the cheaper cars, or offered as a no-cost option on the more expensive grades. Even after the 200D, 250T and 240D lwb models had been dropped, thanks to the 300D lwb being added to the range, there were still 15 cars in the 123 series line-up, ranging in price from £9130 for a 4MT 200 saloon, all the way up to £16,500 for the long-wheelbase variants; the 280CE coupé was the flagship of the regular cars, listed at £14,830, although the real king was the 500SEC, which commanded £28,700 – a full £8000 more than a V12 Jaguar XJ-S HE.

From January 1983, the range was reduced slightly Down Under to include the 230E saloon at $38,450, the 300D saloon at $39,875, the 280E saloon at $46,325, the 300TD estate at $47,360, the 280CE coupé at $50,530, and the 280TE estate

Japanese advertising from mid-1983 showing a limited edition (80-off) 300DT saloon. Finished in white with leather trim, all cars had the special grille badge.

at $51,380. Interestingly, the estate models were allowed to fizzle out after this, until the line was revived via a single 230TE variant, first introduced to the Australian market in December 1983 as a 1984 model.

In Japan, while prices had gone down for 1982, they were back up again for the 1983 season, although the 123 series range was extended thanks to the introduction of the 230E and 300TDT models.

Inside this Mercedes-Benz saloon there's a sports car waiting to get out.

BLF 390Y

British advertising from the spring of 1983.

With the flagship of the range being the 380SEC, the 123 series cars (all with automatic transmission) cost roughly half – the 300DT saloon was listed at ¥5,990,000, the 230E at ¥6,240,000, the 280E at ¥7,290,000, the 300TDT at ¥7,440,000 (significantly more than the old normally-aspirated model), and the 280CE at ¥8,075,000.

The 1984 model year

While domestic prices had increased by around one per cent in July 1983, they rose again at the start of the 1984 season, this time by a further three per cent. This took the price of entry into the 18-car 123 series range up to DM 26,881, but in January, it leapt to DM 27,508 as another two per cent hike was applied.

There were a few mechanical changes made at the start of the 1984 season, including the adoption of the intake manifold from the W201 model on the M102 engine, along with a fresh four-speed manual gearbox for the four-cylinder cars, and a revised automatic transmission on the 280E variants. The 200D- and 240D-based cars got the GL68/20E (type 716.214), the 200- and 230E-based machines inherited the GL68/20F model (716.215), and the automatic 280Es were now fitted with the W4B040 type 722.300 unit. The GL68/20E units came with revised internal ratios of 4.23, 2.36, 1.49 and 1.00, while the 20F version had cogs giving 3.91, 2.17, 1.37 and 1.00; final-drive ratios were unchanged in both cases. As for the automatic, the only changes were refinements to give smoother shifts, so the leading specifications were unaltered.

Left and above: Three 123 series taxi variants, and special version models, mainly for the emergency services, although the white car is a bulletproof model. All had their own SA codes to keep specifications uniform.

An integrated luggage rack became available for estate models in February 1984 (option code SA 722), while on the corporate front, following the death of Gerhard Prinz at the end of 1983, Professor Werner Breitschwerdt became Chairman, and Dr Rudolf Hörnig took over as head of R&D, in May 1984. Hörnig's appointment coincided with a German metalworkers' strike, which put a halt to production for quite some time.

In the States, the 240D was dropped to make way for the new 190 models, and 5-litre S-Class models took the place of the 380s (except in the case of the SL). Just three 123 series cars

W123 and W201 models on the line at Sindelfingen.

survived the reshuffle – the entry-level $31,940 300DT saloon, the 300CDT coupé, and the 300TDT station wagon; a power sunroof was now classed as a no-cost option on the two- and four-door machines, while a manually-operated one was there for free on the $35,310 estates. Although there was another sales record set, the number of diesel buyers fell off sharply thanks to the popularity of the 190, accounting for only half of the 79,222 cars sold – three out of every four Mercedes' sold in the US in 1983 had been oil burners.

Not much change in Britain for 1984, with the 190 and 190E taking up the mantle once held by the W123 200. Actually, the 190E was a fraction more expensive than the £9965 200 saloon, which had gone up by around £800 over the course of a year. The 250 saloon had been dropped by now, but otherwise the UK 123 series line-up was carried over from the 1983 season.

Only five W123-based machines were listed in Australia for 1984, with the 230E saloon at $39,740, the 300D saloon at $40,265, the 280E saloon at $47,450, the 230TE estate at $500 more than the flagship sedan, and the 280CE coupé topping the range at $51,620. Further north, the same five cars were fielded in Japan, and at similar prices to the year before.

Above and top: The US-spec 300DT for 1984, with a look at the car's rear seating. The curvature in the backrest had been revised during the 'Series 3' upgrade.

Continued page 162

Above and opposite: The American 300TDT, this car having a
split rear seat.

Above and right: The 300CDT for the US 1984 season, with views of the model's front and rear seating arrangements.

THE MERCEDES-BENZ 230E

Makes the highest mileage a lot less wearing.

The Mercedes-Benz 230E wears wonderfully well.

The doors go on shutting precisely, with the same satisfying firm 'clunk' that they had in the showroom when brand new.

The seats remain comfortable and firm. The trim, immaculate. The engine smooth, responsive and reliable.

It's simply because Mercedes-Benz engineer longevity into the very structure of the car.

(Those satisfying 'clunks', for example, happen consistently because every single door is individually adjusted so it fits precisely. As is every single boot-lid. And every single bonnet).

The 230E won't wear you out either. Superb ergonomics help you to enjoy the longest journeys in comfort and safety.

The driving position is designed with all the most vital hand controls at fingertip-reach.

At speed, fresh air circulates through the interior and can be completely changed every 20 seconds, keeping the driver refreshed and alert.

The seats are specially designed to support your bodyweight at the pelvic bones, thus avoiding any constriction of blood vessels and risk of dangerous drowsiness.

The highest standards of active and passive safety combine with unsurpassed spaciousness, luxury, reliability, and effortless driving pleasure.

The 230E shares its bodyshell with four other models: the petrol-engined 200 and 280E, and the 240D and 300D, which have diesel engines. Prices begin at £10,365 for the 200.

They all offer you all-round excellence. Which includes, at the end of long and faithful service, and almost in spite of the mileage, a gratifyingly good resale value.

Mercedes-Benz
Engineered like no other car in the world.

Above and opposite: Two pieces of British advertising from 1984, with both of them showing the 230E saloon.

⊛ THE MERCEDES-BENZ 230E

Mercedes-Benz spend over a million pounds a day, seven days a week, on research and development in areas related to safety, environmental factors, noise-reduction and greater efficiency, as well as the very latest advances in electronic and mechanical automotive technology.

Which is how cars like the Mercedes-Benz 230E remain so under-statedly elegant, so quietly efficient. And so very far ahead.

The 230E embodies the Mercedes-Benz philosophy that every aspect of a car should be truly excellent.

So, for example, the 230E offers you long-legged comfort as well as agile manoeuvrability.

And it offers unparalleled standards of safety – a very special pre-occupation with Daimler-Benz.

We built our first experimental safety car in the 1930s, and by 1951 had patented the concept of the "safety-cell", with a rigid passenger compartment and progressively collapsible front, rear and side impact zones.

The 230E shares its bodyshell with four other models: the petrol-engined 200 and 280E, and the 240D and 300D, which have diesel engines.

They all have an enviable record of long, trouble-free life, because quality is engineered into every component. The better a car is built, the better it is likely to perform over time. So we build cars to the highest possible standards.

You'll discover just how high those standards are when you drive a 230E. And what a lasting pleasure they can be.

Our investment is a million pounds a day. The rewards will be all yours.

It costs us a million pounds a day to stay so far ahead.

Mercedes-Benz
Engineered like no other car in the world.

The 200-series offers five engine options: 4 cylinder 1,997cc, fuel-injected 4 cylinder 2,299cc, fuel-injected 6 cylinder 2,746cc, 4 cylinder diesel 2,399cc and 5 cylinder diesel 2,998cc. Prices from £10,365, for the 200.

The 1985 model year

In preparation for the W124 (a car we will look at briefly in the next chapter) coming online, the 123 series was treated to a new coachwork colour palette for 1985, although the trim options remained unchanged. All cars (except the coupés) now came with front seatbelt pretensioners, along with revised seatbelt buckles not long after the season started; new valve seat inserts were adopted on the M102 engine to allow it to deal with lead-free petrol that much better, and particulate filters (or trap oxidizers as they are sometimes known) were employed on the diesel cars. Other than the fitment of more powerful speakers, a different wind deflector made of aluminium for the optional sunroof, and a revised jack sourced from Bilstein, there were no other changes for the 1985 Model Year.

The German range was given a new price list in September 1984, just in time for the 1985 season. The line-up was carried over, but the cost of Mercedes motoring increased yet again: the

The W123 had evolved into a classy machine, full of up-to-the-minute safety ideas and styling – with the help of the 'Series 3' changes – that had stood the test of time well.

Catalogue image showing safety features, including the brake pad wear indicator, seatbelt pretensioner system, airbag, the patented door locks, and ABS light. The top left-hand picture also gives us a useful view of the economy gauge that was introduced on petrol-engined cars with the 'Series 3' run.

Die Bremsbelag-Verschleiß-Anzeige weist Sie rechtzeitig auf den fälligen Belagwechsel hin.

Die Funktionsweise des auf Wunsch erhältlichen, elektronisch gesteuerten Rückhaltesystems Airbag und Gurtstrammer.

Das Sicherheitszapfenschloß widersteht auch stärksten Stößen.

Das auf Wunsch lieferbare Anti-Blockier-System (ABS) sorgt auch auf nasser, schneeglatter oder vereister Fahrbahn für optimale Bremswirkung bei Erhaltung der Lenkfähigkeit.

British advertising from the spring of 1985.

200 saloon now cost DM 28,329; the 230E saloon DM 31,749; the 250 saloon DM 33,288; the 280E saloon DM 39,900; the 200D saloon DM 28,887; the 240D saloon DM 30,780; the 300D saloon DM 33,402; the 200T estate DM 32,661; the 230TE estate DM 36,081; the 280TE estate DM 44,175; the 240TD estate DM 35,112; the 300TD estate DM 37,734; the 300TDT estate DM 44,802; the 230CE coupé DM 37,506; the 280CE coupé DM 44,460; the 250 lwb model DM 49,476; the 240D lwb model DM 47,025; the 300D lwb model DM 49,647; the 230E special purpose chassis DM 30,210; the 250 lwb special purpose chassis DM 36,537; the 240D special purpose chassis DM 29,412; the 240D lwb special purpose chassis DM 34,086; and the 300D lwb special purpose chassis DM 36,708.

An interesting option was made available to home market buyers – a closed-loop catalytic converter. Although the 230E was the only 123 series car that could be specified with this DM 2622 option (which was combined with a lower compression ratio on the engine to allow the use of regular unleaded fuel), it was an interesting move, pointing the way for others to follow in a world that suddenly became aware of the 'Green' side of automotive engineering. Around 1000 W123s were fitted with a cat.

Meanwhile, the final domestic price increase applied to the 123 series cars in April 1985. While the 200D fell by the wayside, the cost of the remaining saloons stayed the same; that of the estate range, the pair of coupés and the lwb models, however, went up by around three per cent. The coupés disappeared from the production lines not long after, in August, bringing about the end of the 300CDT as a result; as it happens, the other export only car – the 300DT – was dropped at the same time. Most of the W123 saloons limped on into November 1985, but it wasn't until January 1986 that the last of the estates were built at the Bremen plant, as a replacement was slow in coming compared to W124 saloon offerings.

In America, things continued as before for the 1985 Model Year, but with ceramic particulate filters fitted to the diesels. The turbo-diesel models shipped to the US received beefier torque converters, and a taller 2.88:1 rear axle ratio (previously 3.07:1 in the States). ABS, whilst made standard on several Mercedes models for 1985, was not added to the 123 series cars. MBNA recorded another year of record sales, but this time around, the W123-based machines accounted for only a small part of the success.

In Britain, the 1985 Model Year price list was issued in October 1984. In a range spanning from £10,070 to £33,420, the 123 series models included the 200 saloon at £10,365, the 240D saloon at £11,170, the 230E saloon at £11,525, the 300D saloon at £12,870, the 280E saloon at £14,995, the 200T estate at £11,290, the 240TD estate at £12,600, the 230TE estate at £13,410, the 300TD estate at £13,680, the 280TE estate at £16,600, the 230CE coupé at £13,545, the 280CE coupé at £17,010, and the 250 lwb model at £19,425. An automatic gearbox was £388 on the four-cylinder petrol cars, or £750 on the diesels; it was a no-cost option on the sixes. Prices increased by almost 20 per cent in the UK at the end of 1985, but the six 123 series cars still on offer were by then the last of the line.

While Japan continued with the same five cars as before, with the price-tag reduced a touch thanks to exchange rate fluctuations, the 1985 season witnessed some huge price increases in Australia, with the saloons having around $10,000 added to their 1984 window stickers (almost $12,000 in the case of the 280E), largely to make marketing space for the smaller 190E – introduced in December 1984 at a lofty $46,425. Keeping

Tailpiece. The 123 series had certainly served Daimler-Benz well, with almost 2,700,000 being built in the end ...

in line with this move, the cost of 280CE motoring went up to $64,513 for 1985, and the 230TE's price increased to $60,425. However, with the introduction of the W124 series in January 1986, prices went even higher, although in all fairness, the new 300E was still less than half the asking price of the $163,000 560SEL. The 300E was joined by 230E and 300D saloons from the off, although the W123 estate limped on for a little longer, before also being superceded by fresh W124 variants. We take a look at those in the next chapter ...

8

The W124 series

The highly-respected W123 and its numerous variants had been a remarkable sales success for Daimler-Benz, although its replacement – the 124 series – would ultimately go on to outsell its predecessor if all model types are taken into consideration ...

Design work on the W124 came together during 1981, closely following the styling cues established by the smaller W201 compact cars. This wasn't a bad thing, as they looked extremely modern compared to the outgoing model, which, to be perfectly honest, was starting to look a little dated by the mid-1980s. Compared to the W123, sharper yet still organic lines were adopted, the nose was smoother and angled back to help it cut through the air easier, the bumpers were more integrated, the window graphics far cleaner, and the bootlid shaped to allow a lower load height when using the luggage compartment. Other details like the trick windscreen wiper arrangement and smooth wheel faces screamed modernity.

Just as importantly, through clever construction techniques, the new car was lighter than its predecessor, a good deal safer thanks to an extra decade of R&D work, and possessed an aerodynamic efficiency that Friedrich Geiger could only dream about. With a Cd figure of 0.30, this was a staggering leap forward, while the interior was essentially a modern interpretation of the W123 cockpit, with sharper lines much in evidence, but the same basic layout.

Mechanically, the M102 engines from the 200 and 230E models were carried over, but the two M103 sixes were new, giving birth to the 260E and 300E variants. On the diesel front, there was a 2-litre four from the 190D, a five-cylinder 2.5-litre

A 230E saloon attracting attention at the 1985 Frankfurt Show.

unit, and a 3-litre six. The chassis components were based quite heavily on W201 practice, with the multi-link rear suspension giving an excellent compromise between ride quality and dynamic handling.

The first prototypes hit the road in the summer of 1982, with 60 cars undergoing a typically severe test programme that allowed pilot production to begin in March 1984, which in turn prompted another series of tests. The company decided to avoid launching the model at the 1984 Frankfurt Show in September, and instead – as had been the habit on earlier medium-class lines – to release the W124 a few months later, in January.

Expansion

A 2-litre fuel-injected powerplant was introduced for markets like Italy, Greece and Portugal, with heavy taxes on cars with larger engines, during the spring of 1985. Ultimately, the 200E that was spawned from this was sold in other places, too, adding a fourth petrol engine to the W124 range in due course, while special purpose chassis versions for coachbuilders expanded the base car line-up.

When the 1985 Frankfurt Show opened its doors for business, all three model families – the C-Class, E-Class and S-Class (including the SL) – had been overhauled, and new technologies, such as ASD (an automatic locking differential), ASR (an early form of traction control) and 4MATIC (an automatic four-wheel drive system) had been presented to the public. Rightfully proud of its traditional engineering, Daimler-Benz had shown it was capable of moving with the times, taking advantage of the latest electronics wizardry.

For fans of the 123 series, of course, the Frankfurt event was to spell the beginning of the end, for the estate version of the W124 was on display. Most of the engines were carried over from the saloons, although the estate was given a 143bhp 3-litre turbo-diesel unit. Also following on from the Frankfurt event, the four-wheel drive 260E 4MATIC and 300E 4MATIC variants eventually made it into showrooms during the spring of 1987, followed soon after by the 300TE 4MATIC and 300TD Turbo 4MATIC estates.

In the meantime, the W124-based coupés were introduced at the 1987 Geneva Show, riding on a shorter wheelbase, just as their predecessors had. In fact, the concept was much the same, with the looks dictated by those of the donor car, but with two doors, a stylish roof and 2+2 seating. A unique feature, however, was the side cladding added low down between the wheels on the coupé models, initially sold in 230CE and 300CE guise.

On the corporate front, Edzard Reuter replaced Werner Beritschwerdt as Chairman a few months later. At the 1987 Frankfurt Show, new diesel engines were announced for W201 and W124 series cars, including the turbo-diesel unit for the saloon, and the W126 series was given uprated V8 engines.

An early W124 saloon, readily identified by its black door mirrors, flanked by a C124 coupé (nearest the camera) and S124 estate.

Interior of one of the first two-door models.

In the following year, the 250D Turbo engine was announced for the saloon at the 1988 Paris Salon, along with the official adoption of the 200E and 200TE models, while ABS braking was made standard for all 124 series cars for the 1989 season.

Face-lift

The 1989 Frankfurt Show witnessed the unveiling of the face-lifted 124 series, with minor styling changes and a subtly revised interior. The main difference on the outside was the adoption of the side cladding first seen on the coupés (but now adopted across the board and dressed with a chrome strip along the top edge that then continued into the bumpers), colour-keyed door mirrors and chrome flashes in the door handles; but the optional Sportline package also lowered the suspension and added a racier wheel and tyre combination.

There was also a new four-valve per cylinder engine, giving birth to the luxurious 300CE-24, while June 1990 saw the export-only 200CE and 250TD Turbo models take a bow. Meanwhile, the long-wheelbase variants had entered production, developed in conjunction with Binz of Lorch, but they paled in comparison with the 500E saloon, launched at the 1990 Paris Salon. Built with the help of Stuttgart neighbour Porsche, this DM 135,000

machine came with the 5-litre V8 from the contemporary SL, and features such as flared wheelarches over 16in alloys, and integral foglights in a lowered front air dam.

Next up was the first four-seater convertible to come from Daimler-Benz since the last of the W111-based models had been built in mid-1971. Launched in September 1991, the 300CE-24 Convertible used the coupé bodyshell as its starting point, suitably stiffened after the loss of its roof panel, and came with a cloth soft top that folded flat behind the rear seats when not in use.

With over 2,000,000 cars already in use, for 1993, the 124 series received a second and final face-lift. Although equipment enhancements were made, this was basically an overhaul of the powertrains, with the M111 engines replacing the M102 units (linked to a five-speed manual gearbox as standard), the M104 replacing the majority of the M103 sixes, and the introduction of a range of four-valve per cylinder diesels. Naturally, model designations were changed in line with the revised engine displacements, while there was also a 400E for the American and Japanese markets offered at this time.

From June 1993, face-lifted cars were christened E-Class models and came with a new grille design, indicator units, a

A W124 saloon following the first (1989) face-lift, identified by its side cladding combined with black bumper inserts.

revised bootlid on the saloons (carrying new badging to suit the latest nomenclature), a power top for convertibles (previously an option), body-coloured bumpers, and a fresh line of wheel designs.

Three months later, the high-performance E36 AMG models were introduced, with a tuned 3.6-litre engine, a bodykit and 17in alloys, while at the other end of the scale, the formally export-only E200 Convertible and E200 Coupé were offered in the domestic market from 1994 to lower the price of entry for younger buyers.

The replacement for the W124 (the W210) was unveiled in June 1995, signalling the imminent end of the old car. Saloon production finished officially in August 1995 (although a few were built as CKD units in India afterwards), the coupé run came to an end in March 1996, a month after the last estate was built at the Bremen plant, and the convertible soldiered on into the summer of 1997. After 12 years, a total of almost 2,750,000 124 series cars had been built.

The E200 Convertible of 1994 vintage. Note the badging on the tail, along with the body-coloured bumpers, pointing to this being a late car.

One of the last saloons, with body-coloured bumpers, the different grille arrangement, and clear indicator lights giving the best form of dating up front (they were traditional amber units before June 1993).

Appendix I

Year-by-year range details

The author usually arranges sections like this by Model Year (MY), but considering the strange mix of launch dates on the W123 models, it is easier to list the various cars in Calendar Year (CY) order according to domestic release dates. The first column shows the model grade and its chassis code, the second the engine code on German cars (to be used in conjunction with Appendix II, with export market specifications covered in the main chapters), while the third contains any notes of relevance.

1975

Model	Engine	Notes
280 (123.030)	110.923	Pilot build from July 1975. Full-scale production starts November 1975.
280E (123.033)	110.984	Pilot build from July 1975. Full-scale production starts November 1975.

1976

Model	Engine	Notes
200 (123.020)	115.938	Pilot build from July 1975. Full-scale production starts February 1976.
230 (123.023)	115.954	Pilot build from July 1975. Full-scale production starts February 1976.
230 SpCh (123.000)	115.954	From July 1976.
250 (123.026)	123.920	Pilot build from July 1975. Full-scale production starts April 1976.
250 LoSpCh (123.003)	123.920	From July 1976.
280 (123.030)	110.923	
280E (123.033)	110.984	
200D (123.120)	615.940	Pilot build from July 1975. Full-scale production starts February 1976.
220D (123.126)	615.941	Pilot build from July 1975. Full-scale production starts February 1976.
240D (123.123)	616.912	Pilot build from July 1975. Full-scale production starts February 1976.
240D SpCh (123.102)	616.912	From July 1976.
240D LoSpCh (123.103)	616.912	From July 1976.
300D (123.130)	617.912	Pilot build from July 1975. Full-scale production starts February 1976.
300D LoSpCh (123.105)	617.912	From July 1976.

1977

Model	Engine	Notes
200 (123.020)	115.938	
230 (123.023)	115.954	
230 SpCh (123.000)	115.954	
230C (123.043)	115.954	Pilot build from November 1976. Full-scale production starts June 1977.
250 (123.026)	123.920	
250 Lang (123.028)	123.920	From September 1977.
250 LoSpCh (123.003)	123.920	
280 (123.030)	110.923	
280E (123.033)	110.984	
280E LoSpCh (123.007)	110.984	From October 1977. Export only.
280C (123.050)	110.923	Pilot build from November 1976. Full-scale production starts April 1977.
280CE (123.053)	110.984	Pilot build from October 1976. Full-scale production starts April 1977.
200D (123.120)	615.940	
220D (123.126)	615.941	
240D (123.123)	616.912	
240D Lang (123.125)	616.912	From September 1977.
240D SpCh (123.102)	616.912	
240D LoSpCh (123.103)	616.912	
300D (123.130)	617.912	
300D Lang (123.132)	617.912	From September 1977.
300D LoSpCh (123.105)	617.912	

Model	Engine	Notes
300CD (123.150)	617.912	Pilot build from May 1977. Full-scale production starts September 1977. Export only.

1978

Model	Engine	Notes
200 (123.020)	115.938	
230 (123.023)	115.954	
230 SpCh (123.000)	115.954	
230T (123.083)	115.954	Pilot build from February 1978. Full-scale production starts April 1978.
230C (123.043)	115.954	
250 (123.026)	123.920	
250 Lang (123.028)	123.920	
250 LoSpCh (123.003)	123.920	
250T (123.086)	123.920	Pilot build from September 1977. Full-scale production starts April 1978.
280 (123.030)	110.923	
280E (123.033)	110.984	To April 1978.
280E (123.033)	110.988	From April 1978.
280E LoSpCh (123.007)	110.984	Export only. To April 1978.
280E LoSpCh (123.007)	110.988	Export only. From April 1978.
280TE (123.093)	110.988	Pilot build from September 1977. Full-scale production starts April 1978.
280C (123.050)	110.923	
280CE (123.053)	110.984	To April 1978.
280CE (123.053)	110.988	From April 1978.
200D (123.120)	615.940	
220D (123.126)	615.941	
240D (123.123)	616.912	Engine revised August 1978.
240D Lang (123.125)	616.912	Engine revised August 1978.
240D SpCh (123.102)	616.912	Engine revised August 1978.
240D LoSpCh (123.103)	616.912	Engine revised August 1978.
240TD (123.183)	616.912	Pilot build from February 1978. Full-scale production starts April 1978. Engine revised August 1978.
300D (123.130)	617.912	Engine revised August 1978.
300D Lang (123.132)	617.912	Engine revised August 1978.
300D LoSpCh (123.105)	617.912	Engine revised August 1978.
300TD (123.190)	617.912	Pilot build from September 1977. Full-scale production starts April 1978. Engine revised August 1978.
300CD (123.150)	617.912	Export only. Engine revised August 1978.

1979

Model	Engine	Notes
200 (123.020)	115.938	
230 (123.023)	115.954	
230 SpCh (123.000)	115.954	
230T (123.083)	115.954	
230C (123.043)	115.954	
250 (123.026)	123.920	To September 1979.
250 (123.026)	123.921	From September 1979.
250 Lang (123.028)	123.920	To September 1979.
250 Lang (123.028)	123.921	From September 1979.
250 LoSpCh (123.003)	123.920	To September 1979.
250 LoSpCh (123.003)	123.921	From September 1979.

250T (123.086)	123.920	To September 1979.		October 1979. Full-scale production starts June 1980.
250T (123.086)	123.921	From September 1979.		
280 (123.030)	110.923		230 SpCh (123.000)	115.954	To June 1980.
280E (123.033)	110.988		230E SpCh (123.200)	102.980	From June 1980.
280E LoSpCh (123.007)	110.988	Export only.	230T (123.083)	115.954	To June 1980.
280TE (123.093)	110.988		230TE (123.283)	102.980	Pilot build from October 1979. Full-scale production starts June 1980.
280C (123.050)	110.923			
280CE (123.053)	110.988			
200D (123.120)	615.940	Engine revised February 1979.	230C (123.043)	115.954	To June 1980.
220D (123.126)	615.941	To March 1979.	230CE (123.243)	102.980	Pilot build from February 1980. Full-scale production starts June 1980.
240D (123.123)	616.912			
240D Lang (123.125)	616.912			
240D SpCh (123.102)	616.912			
240D LoSpCh (123.103)	616.912		250 (123.026)	123.921	
240TD (123.183)	616.912		250 Lang (123.028)	123.921	
300D (123.130)	617.912	Engine revised September 1979.	250 LoSpCh (123.003)	123.921	
			250T (123.086)	123.921	
300D Lang (123.132)	617.912	Engine revised September 1979.	280 (123.030)	110.923	
			280E (123.033)	110.988	
300D LoSpCh (123.105)	617.912	Engine revised September 1979.		
300TD (123.190)	617.912	Engine revised September 1979.		
300CD (123.150)	617.912	Export only. Engine revised September 1979.		

1980

200 (123.020)	115.938	To August 1980.
200 (123.220)	102.920	Pilot build from October 1979. Full-scale production starts August 1980.
200T (123.280)	102.920	Pilot build from May 1980. Full-scale production starts November 1980.
230 (123.023)	115.954	To June 1980.
230E (123.223)	102.980	Pilot build from

Model	Engine	Notes
280E LoSpCh (123.007)	110.988	Export only.
280TE (123.093)	110.988	
280C (123.050)	110.923	To March 1980.
280CE (123.053)	110.988	
200D (123.120)	615.940	
240D (123.123)	616.912	
240D Lang (123.125)	616.912	
240D SpCh (123.102)	616.912	
240D LoSpCh (123.103)	616.912	
240TD (123.183)	616.912	
300D (123.130)	617.912	
300D Lang (123.132)	617.912	
300D LoSpCh (123.105)	617.912	
300TD (123.190)	617.912	
300TDT (123.193)	617.952	Pilot build from November 1979. Full-scale production starts October 1980. Export only.
300CD (123.150)	617.912	

1981

Model	Engine	Notes
200 (123.220)	102.920	
200T (123.280)	102.920	
230E (123.223)	102.980	
230E SpCh (123.200)	102.980	
230TE (123.283)	102.980	
230CE (123.243)	102.980	
250 (123.026)	123.921	
250 Lang (123.028)	123.921	
250 LoSpCh (123.003)	123.921	
250T (123.086)	123.921	
280 (123.030)	110.923	To July 1981.
280E (123.033)	110.988	
280E LoSpCh (123.007)	110.988	Export only.
280TE (123.093)	110.988	
280CE (123.053)	110.988	
200D (123.120)	615.940	
240D (123.123)	616.912	
240D Lang (123.125)	616.912	
240D SpCh (123.102)	616.912	
240D LoSpCh (123.103)	616.912	

Model	Engine	Notes
240TD (123.183)	616.912	
300D (123.130)	617.912	
300DT (123.133)	617.952	Pilot build from April 1981. Full-scale production starts August 1981. Export only.
300D Lang (123.132)	617.912	
300D LoSpCh (123.105)	617.912	
300TD (123.190)	617.912	
300TDT (123.193)	617.952	
300CD (123.150)	617.912	Export only. To August 1981.
300CDT (123.153)	617.952	Export only. From August 1981.

1982

Model	Engine	Notes
200 (123.220)	102.920	
200T (123.280)	102.920	
230E (123.223)	102.980	
230E SpCh (123.200)	102.980	
230TE (123.283)	102.980	
230CE (123.243)	102.980	
250 (123.026)	123.921	
250 Lang (123.028)	123.921	
250 LoSpCh (123.003)	123.921	
250T (123.086)	123.921	To August 1982.
280E (123.033)	110.988	
280E LoSpCh (123.007)	110.988	Export only.
280TE (123.093)	110.988	
280CE (123.053)	110.988	
200D (123.120)	615.940	
240D (123.123)	616.912	
240D Lang (123.125)	616.912	
240D SpCh (123.102)	616.912	
240D LoSpCh (123.103)	616.912	
240TD (123.183)	616.912	
300D (123.130)	617.912	
300DT (123.133)	617.952	Export only.
300D Lang (123.132)	617.912	
300D LoSpCh (123.105)	617.912	

300TD (123.190)	617.912		300TD (123.190)	617.912	
300TDT (123.193)	617.952		300TDT (123.193)	617.952	
300CDT (123.153)	617.952	Export only.	300CDT (123.153)	617.952	Export only.

1983 / **1984**

200 (123.220)	102.920		200 (123.220)	102.920	
200T (123.280)	102.920		200T (123.280)	102.920	
230E (123.223)	102.980		230E (123.223)	102.980	
230E SpCh (123.200)	102.980		230E SpCh (123.200)	102.980	
230TE (123.283)	102.980		230TE (123.283)	102.980	
230CE (123.243)	102.980		230CE (123.243)	102.980	
250 (123.026)	123.921		250 (123.026)	123.921	
250 Lang (123.028)	123.921		250 Lang (123.028)	123.921	
250 LoSpCh (123.003)	123.921		250 LoSpCh (123.003)	123.921	
280E (123.033)	110.988		280E (123.033)	110.988	
280E LoSpCh (123.007)	110.988	Export only.	280E LoSpCh (123.007)	110.988	Export only.
280TE (123.093)	110.988		280TE (123.093)	110.988	
280CE (123.053)	110.988		280CE (123.053)	110.988	
200D (123.120)	615.940		200D (123.120)	615.940	
240D (123.123)	616.912		240D (123.123)	616.912	
240D Lang (123.125)	616.912		240D Lang (123.125)	616.912	
240D SpCh (123.102)	616.912		240D SpCh (123.102)	616.912	
240D LoSpCh (123.103)	616.912		240D LoSpCh (123.103)	616.912	
240TD (123.183)	616.912		240TD (123.183)	616.912	
300D (123.130)	617.912		300D (123.130)	617.912	
300DT (123.133)	617.952	Export only.	300DT (123.133)	617.952	Export only.
300D Lang (123.132)	617.912		300D Lang (123.132)	617.912	
300D LoSpCh (123.105)	617.912		300D LoSpCh (123.105)	617.912	

300TD (123.190)	617.912		250 (123.026)	123.921	To December 1985.
300TDT (123.193)	617.952		250 Lang (123.028)	123.921	To December 1985.
300CDT (123.153)	617.952	Export only.	250 LoSpCh (123.003)	123.921	To October 1985.
			280E (123.033)	110.988	To December 1985.
1985			280E LoSpCh (123.007)	110.988	Export only. To December 1985.
200 (123.220)	102.920	To November 1985.			
200T (123.280)	102.920		280TE (123.093)	110.988	
230E (123.223)	102.980	To November 1985.	280CE (123.053)	110.988	To August 1985.
230E SpCh (123.200)	102.980	To October 1985.	200D (123.120)	615.940	To April 1985.
230TE (123.283)	102.980		240D (123.123)	616.912	To November 1985.
230CE (123.243)	102.980	To August 1985.	240D Lang (123.125)	616.912	To November 1985.

240D SpCh (123.102)	616.912	To October 1985.	300CDT (123.153)	617.952	Export only. To August 1985.
240D LoSpCh (123.103)	616.912	To October 1985.			
240TD (123.183)	616.912				
300D (123.130)	617.912	To November 1985.	**1986**		
300DT (123.133)	617.952	Export only. To August 1985.	200T (123.280)	102.920	To January 1986.
			230TE (123.283)	102.980	To January 1986.
300D Lang (123.132)	617.912	To November 1985.	280TE (123.093)	110.988	To January 1986.
300D LoSpCh (123.105)	617.912	To October 1985.	240TD (123.183)	616.912	To January 1986.
300TD (123.190)	617.912		300TD (123.190)	617.912	To January 1986.
300TDT (123.193)	617.952		300TDT (123.193)	617.952	To January 1986.

Note: SpCh = Special-purpose chassis; LoSpCh = Long-wheelbase special-purpose chassis.

Appendix II

Engine specifications

The following is a survey of all the mainstream production engines employed in the 123 series models featured in this book, complete with the leading specifications and any other notes of interest. The figures and code number changes are based on the domestic market situation. As such, some of the dates and specifications may not tie-up with exported machines, although these are all covered in the main text. Note also that the line on usage refers to the saloon designation for ease of reference, but one should also bear in mind that a model line often includes coupé, estate, lwb and chassis-only variants.

Type 102.920 (M102 V20)

Production (MY)	1981-1986
Fuel	Petrol
Cylinders	Straight-four, water-cooled
Main bearings	Five, in cast iron block
Valve operation	Sohc, 8v, in alloy head
Bore & stroke	89.0 x 80.3mm
Cubic capacity	1997cc
Compression ratio	9.0:1
Fuel delivery system	Single Stromberg 175CDT carburettor
Power @ rpm	109bhp (80kW) DIN @ 5200
Torque @ rpm	125lbft (170Nm) DIN @ 3000

Notes: Used in the face-lifted 200 models from August 1980 to January 1986.

The M102 V20 engine.

Type 102.980 (M102 E23)

Production (MY)	1980-1986
Fuel	Petrol
Cylinders	Straight-four, water-cooled
Main bearings	Five, in cast iron block
Valve operation	Sohc, 8v, in alloy head
Bore & stroke	95.5 x 80.3mm
Cubic capacity	2299cc
Compression ratio	9.0:1
Fuel delivery system	Bosch K-Jetronic fuel-injection
Power @ rpm	136bhp (100kW) DIN @ 5100
Torque @ rpm	151lbft (205Nm) DIN @ 3500

Notes: Used in the 230E models from June 1980 to January 1986.

Type 110.923 (M110 V28)

Production (MY)	1976-1981
Fuel	Petrol
Cylinders	Straight-six, water-cooled
Main bearings	Seven, in cast iron block
Valve operation	Dohc, 12v, in alloy head
Bore & stroke	86.0 x 78.8mm
Cubic capacity	2746cc
Compression ratio	8.7:1
Fuel delivery system	Single twin-choke Solex 4A1 carburettor
Power @ rpm	156bhp (115kW) DIN @ 5500
Torque @ rpm	164lbft (223Nm) DIN @ 4000

Notes: Used in the 280 models from December 1975 to July 1981.

Type 110.984 (M110 E28)

Production (MY)	1976-1986
Fuel	Petrol
Cylinders	Straight-six, water-cooled
Main bearings	Seven, in cast iron block
Valve operation	Dohc, 12v, in alloy head
Bore & stroke	86.0 x 78.8mm
Cubic capacity	2746cc
Compression ratio	8.7:1
Fuel delivery system	Bosch K-Jetronic fuel-injection
Power @ rpm	177bhp (130kW) DIN @ 6000
Torque @ rpm	173lbft (234Nm) DIN @ 4500

Notes: Used in the European 280E models from December 1975 to April 1978, but continued to be used in the US and Japan.

The M110 V28 engine.

The M102 E23 engine.

Cubic capacity   2746cc
Compression ratio   9.0:1
Fuel delivery system Bosch K-Jetronic fuel-injection
Power @ rpm   185bhp (136kW) DIN @ 5800
Torque @ rpm   177lbft (240Nm) DIN @ 4500
Notes: Used in the European 280E models from April 1978 to January 1986.

Type 115.938 (M115 V20)

Production (MY)   1976-1980
Fuel   Petrol
Cylinders   Straight-four, water-cooled
Main bearings   Five, in cast iron block
Valve operation   Sohc, 8v, in alloy head
Bore & stroke   87.0 x 83.6mm
Cubic capacity   1988cc
Compression ratio   9.0:1
Fuel delivery system   Single Stromberg 175CDT carburettor
Power @ rpm   94bhp (69kW) DIN @ 4800
Torque @ rpm   117lbft (158Nm) DIN @ 3000
Notes: Used in the 200 models from February 1976 to August 1980.

Type 115.954 (M115 V23)

Production (MY)   1976-1980
Fuel   Petrol
Cylinders   Straight-four, water-cooled
Main bearings   Five, in cast iron block
Valve operation   Sohc, 8v, in alloy head
Bore & stroke   93.8 x 83.6mm
Cubic capacity   2307cc
Compression ratio   9.0:1
Fuel delivery system   Single Stromberg 175CDT carburettor
Power @ rpm   109bhp (80kW) DIN @ 4800
Torque @ rpm   137lbft (186Nm) DIN @ 3000
Notes: Used in the 230 models from February 1976 to August 1980.

Type 123.920 (M123 V25)

Production (MY)   1976-1979
Fuel   Petrol

The M110 E28 engine.

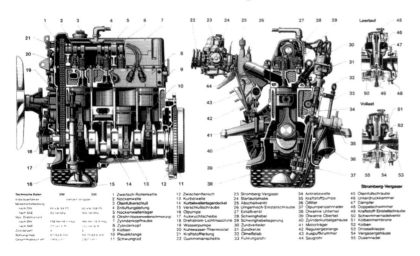

The M115 V20 and V23 engine.

Type 110.988 (M110 E28)

Production (MY)   1978-1986
Fuel   Petrol
Cylinders   Straight-six, water-cooled
Main bearings   Seven, in cast iron block
Valve operation   Dohc, 12v, in alloy head
Bore & stroke   86.0 x 78.8mm

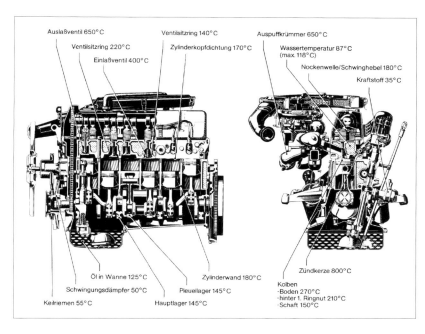

The M123 V25 engine.

Cylinders: Straight-six, water-cooled
Main bearings: Four, in cast iron block
Valve operation: Sohc, 12v, in alloy head
Bore & stroke: 86.0 x 72.5
Cubic capacity: 2525cc
Compression ratio: 8.7:1
Fuel delivery system: Single twin-choke Solex 4A1 carburettor
Power @ rpm: 129bhp (95kW) DIN @ 5500
Torque @ rpm: 145lbft (196Nm) DIN @ 3500

Notes: Used in the 250 models from April 1976 to September 1979.

Type 123.921 (M123 V25)

Production (MY): 1980-1986
Fuel: Petrol
Cylinders: Straight-six, water-cooled
Main bearings: Four, in cast iron block
Valve operation: Sohc, 12v, in alloy head
Bore & stroke: 86.0 x 72.5
Cubic capacity: 2525cc
Compression ratio: 9.0:1
Fuel delivery system: Single twin-choke Solex 4A1 carburettor

Power @ rpm: 140bhp (103kW) DIN @ 5500
Torque @ rpm: 148lbft (200Nm) DIN @ 3500

Notes: Used in the 250 models from September 1979 to December 1985.

Type 615.940 (OM615 D20)

Production (MY): 1976-1985
Fuel: Diesel
Cylinders: Straight-four, water-cooled
Main bearings: Five, in cast iron block
Valve operation: Sohc, 8v, in cast iron head
Bore & stroke: 87.0 x 83.6mm
Cubic capacity: 1988cc
Compression ratio: 21.0:1
Fuel delivery system: Fuel-injection
Power @ rpm: 55bhp (40kW) DIN @ 4200
Torque @ rpm: 83lbft (113Nm) DIN @ 2400

Notes: Used in the 200D models from February 1976 to April 1985. Engine revised February 1979, increasing power to 60bhp (44kW) at 4400rpm.

Type 615.941 (OM615 D22)

Production (MY): 1976-1979
Fuel: Diesel
Cylinders: Straight-four, water-cooled
Main bearings: Five, in cast iron block

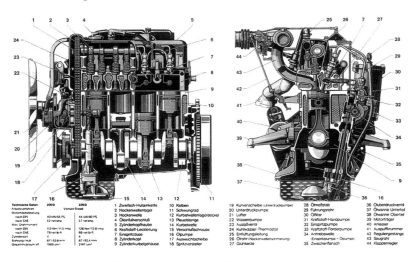

The OM615 D20 and D22 engine.

Valve operation	Sohc, 8v, in cast iron head
Bore & stroke	87.0 x 92.4mm
Cubic capacity	2197cc

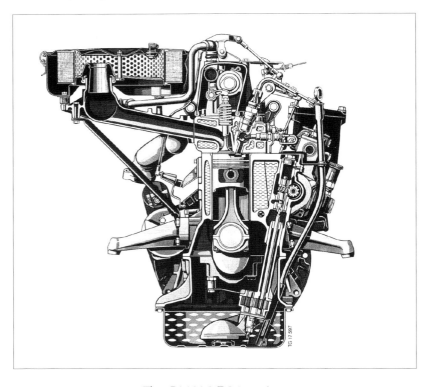

The OM616 D24 engine.

The OM617 D30 engine.

Compression ratio	21.0:1
Fuel delivery system	Fuel-injection
Power @ rpm	60bhp (44kW) DIN @ 4200
Torque @ rpm	93lbft (126Nm) DIN @ 2400

Notes: Used in the 220D models from February 1976 to March 1979.

Type 616.912 (OM616 D24)

Production (MY)	1976-1986
Fuel	Diesel
Cylinders	Straight-four, water-cooled
Main bearings	Five, in cast iron block
Valve operation	Sohc, 8v, in cast iron head
Bore & stroke	91.0 x 92.4mm
Cubic capacity	2404cc
Compression ratio	21.0:1
Fuel delivery system	Fuel-injection
Power @ rpm	65bhp (48kW) DIN @ 4200
Torque @ rpm	101lbft (137Nm) DIN @ 2400

Notes: Used in the 240D models from February 1976 to January 1986. Engine revised August 1978, with bore adjusted to 90.9mm to give a 2399cc displacement. Power increased to 72bhp (53kW) at 4400rpm at the same time.

Type 617.912 (OM617 D30)

Production (MY)	1976-1986
Fuel	Diesel
Cylinders	Straight-five, water-cooled
Main bearings	Six, in cast iron block
Valve operation	Sohc, 10v, in cast iron head
Bore & stroke	91.0 x 92.4mm
Cubic capacity	3005cc
Compression ratio	21.0:1
Fuel delivery system	Fuel-injection
Power @ rpm	80bhp (59kW) DIN @ 4000
Torque @ rpm	127lbft (172Nm) DIN @ 2400

Notes: Used in the 300D models from February 1976 to January 1986. Engine revised August 1978, with bore adjusted to 90.9mm to give a 2998cc displacement. The unit was revised again in September 1979, when power increased to 88bhp (65kW) at 4400rpm.

Type 617.952 (OM617 D30A)

Production (MY)	1981-1986
Fuel	Diesel
Cylinders	Straight-five, water-cooled
Main bearings	Six, in cast iron block
Valve operation	Sohc, 10v, in cast iron head
Bore & stroke	90.9 x 92.4mm
Cubic capacity	2998cc
Compression ratio	21.5:1
Fuel delivery system	Fuel-injection, plus exhaust-driven turbocharger
Power @ rpm	125bhp (92kW) DIN @ 4350
Torque @ rpm	184lbft (250Nm) DIN @ 2400

Notes: Used in the 300DT models from October 1980 to January 1986.

The OM617 D30A engine.

Appendix III

Chassis numbers and production figures

Chassis numbers

Body codes and chassis start numbers for each model, arranged by body style, and engine size/type. Please be careful to read the notes at the bottom of this section, as they have a bearing on prefix usage and what replaces the asterisks; they also cover the VIN system predominantly used in the US:

Saloons	Year	Body code	Chassis no
200 saloon	1976-80	W123.V20	123.020-**-000001
200 saloon	1980-85	W123.V20	123.220-**-000001
230 saloon	1976-80	W123.V23	123.023-**-000001
230E saloon	1980-85	W123.E23	123.223-**-000001
250 saloon	1976-85	W123.V25	123.026-**-000001
250 lwb saloon	1977-85	V123.V25	123.028-**-000001
280 saloon	1975-81	W123.V28	123.030-**-000001
280E saloon	1975-85	W123.E28	123.033-**-000001
200D saloon	1976-85	W123.D20	123.120-**-000001
220D saloon	1976-79	W123.D22	123.126-**-000001
240D saloon	1976-85	W123.D24	123.123-**-000001
240D lwb saloon	1977-85	V123.D24	123.125-**-000001
300D saloon	1976-85	W123.D30	123.130-**-000001
300D lwb saloon	1977-85	V123.D30	123.132-**-000001
300DT saloon	1981-85	W123.D30A	123.133-**-000001

Estates	Year	Body code	Chassis no
200T estate	1980-86	S123.V20	123.280-**-000001
230T estate	1978-80	S123.V23	123.083-**-000001

230TE estate	1980-86	S123.E23	123.283-**-000001
250T estate	1978-82	S123.V25	123.086-**-000001
280TE estate	1978-86	S123.E28	123.093-**-000001
240TD estate	1978-86	S123.D24	123.183-**-000001
300TD estate	1978-86	S123.D30	123.190-**-000001
300TDT estate	1980-86	S123.D30A	123.193-**-000001

Coupés	Year	Body code	Chassis no
230C coupé	1977-80	C123.V23	123.043-**-000001
230CE coupé	1980-85	C123.E23	123.243-**-000001
280C coupé	1977-80	C123.V28	123.050-**-000001
280CE coupé	1977-85	C123.E28	123.053-**-000001
300CD coupé	1977-81	C123.D30	123.150-**-000001
300CDT coupé	1981-85	C123.D30A	123.153-**-000001

Chassis only	Year	Body code	Chassis no
230 chassis	1976-80	F123.V23	123.000-**-000001
230E chassis	1980-85	F123.E23	123.200-**-000001
250 lwb chassis	1976-85	VF123.V25	123.003-**-000001
280E lwb chassis	1977-85	VF123.E28	123.007-**-000001
240D chassis	1976-85	F123.D24	123.102-**-000001
240D lwb chassis	1976-85	VF123.D24	123.103-**-000001
300D lwb chassis	1976-85	VF123.D30	123.105-**-000001

Until the VIN system was introduced in January 1980, chassis numbers started with the digits shown above to differentiate model types, and were followed by a '1' for lhd or '2' for rhd, a '0' for manual cars or '2' for automatics, then a six-figure serial number to tie-in with the build sequence. From January 1980 to August 1983, when the system changed again, a 'WDB' prefix was added to the above codes to give an early style 17-digit VIN number for European cars.

The 1984 Model Year onwards numbers were similar to those issued between 1980 and 1983, with only the digit formally used for the transmission code being used for another purpose, namely a letter ('A' through 'E') to show the car was built in the Sindelfingen plant, or 'F' through 'H' for cars built in Bremen. Build numbers became sequential regardless of model type at this time, resetting to number one in the process.

For America and certain other countries, beginning in 1980, the 17-digit VIN number starts 'WDB' to identify Daimler-Benz. The next four digits describe the model (with 'A' for 123 series, followed by 'A' for a petrol engine or 'B' for a diesel, then a model key, such as '20' which is a shortened version of 123.220). The eighth digit shows restraint systems, and the ninth is simply a check digit, which is a number ('0' to '9') or an 'X' in place of the number ten. The tenth gives the year of manufacture, which is defined by letters (A = 1980, B = 1981, C = 1982, D = 1983, E = 1984, F = 1985, and G = 1986). Next is a letter for the Sindelfingen plant ('A' through 'E') or Bremen ('F' through 'H'), followed by a six-digit sequential serial number.

Production figures

Production quantities for each model, split by body style and engine size:

Saloons	Year	No built
200 saloon	1976-80	158,772
200 saloon	1980-85	217,315
230 saloon	1976-80	195,920
230E saloon	1980-85	245,588
250 saloon	1976-85	114,796
250 lwb saloon	1977-85	5180
280 saloon	1975-81	33,206
280E saloon	1975-85	126,004
200D saloon	1976-85	378,138
220D saloon	1976-79	56,736
240D saloon	1976-85	448,986
240D lwb saloon	1977-85	3841
300D saloon	1976-85	324,718
300D lwb saloon	1977-85	4679
300DT saloon	1981-85	75,261

Coupés	Year	No built
230C coupé	1977-80	18,675
230CE coupé	1980-85	29,858
280C coupé	1977-80	3704
280CE coupé	1977-85	32,138
300CD coupé	1977-81	7502
300CDT coupé	1981-85	8007

Estates	Year	No built
200T estate	1980-86	18,860
230T estate	1978-80	6884
230TE estate	1980-86	42,284
250T estate	1978-82	7704
280TE estate	1978-86	19,789
240TD estate	1978-86	38,903
300TD estate	1978-86	36,874
300TDT estate	1980-86	28,219

Chassis only	Year	No built
230 chassis	1976-80	265
230E chassis	1980-85	294
250 lwb chassis	1976-85	2888
280E lwb chassis	1977-85	371
240D chassis	1976-85	794
240D lwb chassis	1976-85	1159
300D lwb chassis	1976-85	2602

Total number of saloons built	*2,389,140*
Total number of coupés built	*99,884*
Total number of estates built	*199,517*
Total number of chassis built	*8373*

Total 123 series models built	**2,696,914**

Also from Veloce Publishing –

ISBN: 978-1-845841-13-3
Paperback • 19.5x13.9cm • £9.99* UK/$19.95* USA
• 64 pages • 122 colour pictures

ISBN: 978-1-845841-07-2
Paperback • 19.5x13.9cm • £12.99* UK/$25* USA/$30* CAN
• 64 pages • 100 colour pictures

Benefit from the author's years of ownership experience. This step-by-step guide will help you evaluate any example. With 100 photos of what to look for and avoid, plus a realistic assessment of running and restoration costs, as well as market values, you're sure to get the right car at the right price!

For more info on Veloce titles, visit our website at www.veloce.co.uk • email: info@veloce.co.uk • Tel: +44(0)1305 260068
* prices subject to change, p&p extra

Also from Veloce Publishing –

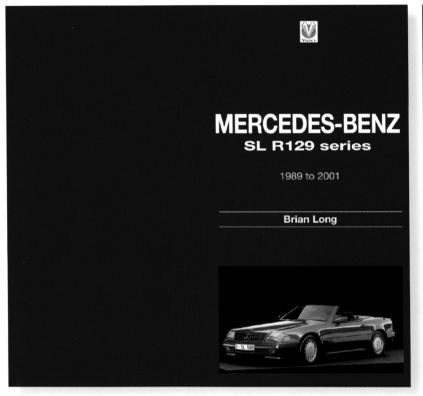

ISBN: 978-1-845844-48-6
Hardback • 25x25cm • £40* UK/$69.95* USA • 208 pages
• 370 colour and b&w pictures

ISBN: 978-1-845847-47-0
Hardback • 25x25cm • £50* UK/$80* USA • 224 pages
• 433 colour and b&w pictures

These detailed and beautifully illustrated books cover several major Mercedes-Benz models, ranging from 1989 to 2011.
Written by a well-respected motoring writer, these are the definitive studies of their subjects.

Also from Veloce Publishing –

ISBN: 978-1-845846-51-0
Hardback • 24.8x24.8cm • £45* UK/$75* USA • 192 pages
• 337 colour pictures

ISBN: 978-1-845846-53-4
Hardback • 24.8x24.8cm • £45* UK/$75* USA • 224 pages
• 388 colour pictures

For more info on Veloce titles, visit our website at www.veloce.co.uk • email: info@veloce.co.uk • Tel: +44(0)1305 260068
* prices subject to change, p&p extra

Also from Veloce Publishing –

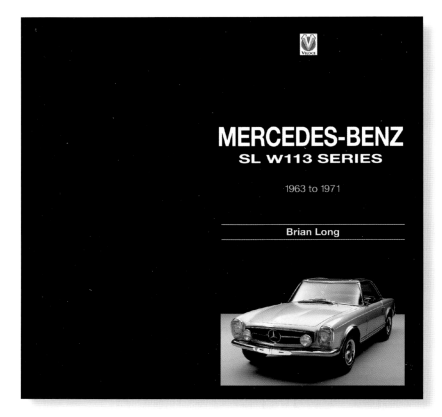

MERCEDES-BENZ
SL W113 SERIES

1963 to 1971

Brian Long

ISBN: 978-1-845843-04-5
Hardback • 25x25cm • £35* UK/$69.95* USA • 208 pages
• 286 colour and b&w pictures

This detailed and beautifully illustrated book covers the Mercedes-Benz W113 series, which ran from 1963 to 1971. Written by a highly regarded motoring writer, with many years' ownership of the Mercedes SL, this is the definitive study of the subject.

For more info on Veloce titles, visit our website at www.veloce.co.uk • email: info@veloce.co.uk • Tel: +44(0)1305 260068
* prices subject to change, p&p extra

Index

Mercedes-Benz, as well as Daimler-Benz and Daimler AG, along with their subsidiaries and
products, are mentioned throughout the book.